DEDICATIONS

This book is dedicated to all the men and women of the Public Safety Department, Metro Dade Police Department and the Miami-Dade Police Department, that served with me from April 1960 until May 1985, in Dade County Florida.

It is also a thank you to all the men and women that have taken over the reins and task of protecting the Highways and By-ways of Dade County Florida, since my retirement.

A special thanks to the City Police Departments of North Miami Beach, Miami Shores, Biscayne Park and El Portal who were always willing to lend a hand when it was necessary to pursue crime within their city limits.

A Very Special Thanks to my wife of 39 years, Chiquita Faye Mensing Palmer, who passed away the morning of our 39th Anniversary, and my son John Robert Palmer that had to give up a lot of things while I was away from home and not able to be with them.

A special thanks to three very fine Ladies, Geraldine Schickler, Irene Shore and Nancy Kerrigan. Three of the best Secretaries that anybody could ever have the pleasure of working with.

(THANK YOU)

To all of the following Officers I worked with in one way or another and helped me make it through 25years. "THANKS"

Gary Adams, Bill Ansley, Sims Arrington, Jim Askew, Rollie Biggs, Dale Bowlin, Ed & Liz Brown, Gary Buchanan, Ellen Carlile, Earl Chantlos,,Bernie Charette, Frank Cliftion, Samuel Duncan, Fred Fauvell, Bernie Goldman, Irving Heller, Art Hill, Paul Huizenga, J. B. Johnson, Joe Johnson, Glen Kay, Frank Kovacs, Tom Lamont, John LeClaire, Bobby Lengel, Pat Leonard, Ron Ludwin, Freddie Maas, Glen Moffit, Irving Nehr, William Powers, Tina & Jim Ratcliff, John Rivera, Dave Rivers, Bill Sandstrom, Robert Senk, Art Stack, Fred Taylor, Joe Thorne, Jim Touchton, Ray Van Billiard, Richard Ward, Ralph Walker, Sam Williams, Buck Wooldridge, & Bill Wright.

To all of the Secretaries that gave so much support to everyone who asked. THANKS. Nancy Kerrigan (Help Us to receive Over-Time Pay), Gerry Schickler (Best of Secretaries) and <u>Irene Shore (My Jewish Mother who kept me straight)</u>

25 YEARS WITH THE MIAMI-DADE POLICE

by Robert J. Palmer

I shall never forget how I obtained my position with the Metro-Dade Police Department. When I first joined the force it was Known as the Public Safety Department. Some people thought from the name that we were an Insurance Company. Some years after I was on the force and the Position of Sheriff became appointed rather than elective and the name was change. This all came about because Dade County applied for and was granted Home Rule Charter from the State of Florida.

I was working one day at a gas station soon after I was separated from active duty with the U S Navy when a friend of mine and high school class mate happened to stop, in the station for gas. He told me that I should apply, for a position with the Department as, they were hiring and I would surely get on as they had just merged the old Sheriff's Road Patrol with The Dade County Parks Police and hence the Public Safety Department was born.

I had to go take a Civil Service test which I did and passed with flying colors as most of the test was based upon your knowledge of Dade County itself. Since I grew up as a teenager from 1949 through my High School Days at good old Miami Edison Senior High School. I graduated from there in June of 1953. I then worked for Margret Ann/ Kwik Check/ Winn Dixie until I joined the navy in 1955.

After passing the Civil Service test with flying colors with my veterans points, of course I was advised to report for an oral interview with Chief Lepigg. I walked in and was asked to see my voters registration card. I explained that I was recently released from active duty with the navy and had not had time to apply for one. They would not, at the time I was in the navy, allow Servicemen to apply or register to vote by mail. I had attempted to register, several times. I was then told go over to the voters registration office a few doors down in the same building called the Metro-Annex. I was told to return after lunch with the voters card and to make sure it had a big D on it. When I arrived at the Annex ,I told the lady behind the desk that I needed to register to vote so I could get a job with the Public Safety Department and to make sure it Had a big D on the card. The lady asked if I wanted to register as a Democrat to which I replied "I do not care as long as it had a big D on it so that I would be hired". I received my card and headed back after lunch for the rest of my interview. I showed the chief my card and he told me right away that I was hired and to report to the Police Academy on Monday April 11, 1960. This would prove to be a real interesting experience. It would last for thirteen weeks.

   I reported to the police academy that Monday and the day started off with PE which consisted of choosing sides and playing tag football. When our first instructor show up about 2 hours late at 10:00 am we had our first class on the Ordinances of Dade County. This lasted for about 45 minutes and then we broke for lunch and told to report back at 1:00 pm for the after noon classes. When we arrived back from lunch the first instructor was late so me played some more tag football. Our State Law instructor arrived around 2:30 pm and taught us the State Statutes for an hour and 15 minutes. We then were told to go home and return at 8:00 am sharp on Tuesday. Well this day also started off with a bang so you guessed it we played more flag football. The instructor finally arrived around 9:45 am and said he was sorry but he had been in court all morning.

We once again started on County Ordinances. We soon learned that this instructor had an explicit vocabulary and every few words should have been beeped out. One student had enough courage to raise his hand and inform the instructor that we had an Ordained Minister in the class and he replied Oh S**T and went out side in a hurry and told us it was football time again.

When we gathered back inside to finish out the morning the Instructor apologized and informed us he would clean up the language from here on out. After an hour we broke for lunch and was told to return at 2:00 pm, for the afternoon session. I think you are starting to get the picture of our first days in the Police Academy.

The rest of the first week was spent on physical fitness via various activities as we were told that we would have to pass a rugged and strict physical agility test before we could graduate from the Police Academy.

In the third week of the Academy we moved from the Miami Springs portable buildings to the Civil Defense Center in South Dade County. This place was like a bomb shelter and could be locked up tight and had supplies to last a few weeks if necessary.

We finished our training on State Statutes, County Ordinances and Traffic Violations. We then moved on to the laws of Search and Seizure and Search Warrants. This was followed by when to make arrests without a warrant and when a warrant was needed before you could make an arrest. This lasted about two weeks. Next we moved on to self defense and learned how to throw each other around and go home with welts and bruises. We learned proper ways to put each other into holds so as to be able to control

a person and make him or her, do what we wanted them to do. We then moved on to a course in how not to wreck a patrol car and to make traffic stops without getting killed in the process.

As the Civil Defense Center was located next to the Fire Department training Center we spent a week learning how to put out fires and assist the fire department when we arrived on a scene with them. This came in handy many times during my three and a half years in Uniform and in the Patrol and Traffic Division. Many times I found myself holding a hose myself after arriving on the scene of a fire and finding only one man on the fire truck. They were very short handed and most fire stations had two trucks, one pumper and one tanker and only three men on duty at the station.

I soon learned it was better to keep your mouth shut and your ears open as we lost one of our classmates within 3 weeks of graduations. It seems that we would have to purchase our own service revolvers and we found out that one classmate had been a firearms dealer and was making us great deals on our future service revolvers. This we found out pissed off a Chief who as it happened was also intending, to sell us our service revolvers, so you can guess what happened from that. Our classmate disappeared and we were told he flunked out ,but we later found out the real truth after we graduated.

Time was getting close to graduation so the physical agility began once again so that we could pass our agility test before graduation. This test consisted of: 25 push ups, 25 jumping jacks, 25 duck walks, 10 foot rope climb, carrying a person on your back in a fireman's carry for fifty yards. This resulted in one guys being carried 25 times as he weighed only 135 pounds and most of the rest of us weighed over 200 lbs. He went home that night with his manhood hurting from all the bouncing up and down on all the shoulders. The rest of the test consisted of four quarters of tag football. Some how we all passed and were sworn in by then Sheriff Thomas Kelly. Sheriff Kelly was one of the last elected Sheriff's of Dade County Florida.

After graduation we were all assigned to various duties and stations. Some went to the North District Station in Carol City, Some went to the South District in Perrine, Some went to the Miami International Airport District which we provided the police services for, Some went to work in the County Jail which at this time was in the top three floors of the Court House in Downtown Miami, and some of us including myself went to the Central District Station working out of the Metro Annex were I had to previously go and register to vote.

I was assigned a veteran officer to break me in on the road and I was assigned to the so called midnight shift from 11PM to 7 am. Since my station was almost downtown we always had to ride quite a district to get to the central part of unincorporated Dade County. At the time I went on the Department there were 26 different Municipalities within Dade County and unless asked to do so, we only patrolled the areas not in one of the cities. This was a challenge in it self to try and learn when you were in the county or when you was in a city.

My training officer, on my first night of duty, told me two things to remember and never forget them. The first was always to know where you was at in case you needed to call for help and the second thing was never to see any thing that happened 45 minutes prior to transfer time, so you could be at the gas pumps and fill your vehicle up and be at the station in time for transfer without having to work overtime. We almost broke the second rule the first Friday on the beat. We received a call in reference to an armed robbery. It seemed, 3 masked men had held up a construction crew as they were being paid from the back of a pick up truck and this occurred at 6:00 am. Needless to say by the time we finished the report and the Robbery Squad arrived on the scene and we arrived back at the Annex for transfer, I had my first 3 hours of overtime which we did not get paid for.

I rode with my first partner for about 3 months until one night I was cut loose on my own. It turn out to be a little scary at first after having a partner but I soon got over it and so of liked the idea that now I could make all of my own decisions.

I remember stopping a vehicle with three black male in it for running a red light at a high rate of speed. The vehicle had an out of county tag (Palm Beach County) on it and I was in the process of writing the driver a ticket for running the red light, when the driver approached my vehicle and handed me a $50.00 bill and asked if I would forget the whole thing. Boy, this sort of stunned me. I told the driver to return to his vehicle and remain inside until I told him what to do. I immediately requested the shift sergeant to my location. Upon his arrival I showed him the fifty and asked him what I should do. He informed me that it was my word against the drivers, but if I were, him I would arrest him for attempted bribery which I ended up doing.

I did not find out until I went to court why he wanted out of the ticket so bad. As it turned out the driver was a big lottery runner in Palm Beach County and was out of jail and on Parole and as part of the conditions of his parole he was not to be outside Palm Beach County. I must have convinced the Judge that I was telling the truth as he was found guilty and given a 5 year sentence in Raiford Prison and would also have more time added on from Palm Beach County for the Parole Violation. I guess that it also helped my case that when the Crime Lab processed the fifty they found his fingerprints on the bill (Gotcha). My first big case was over and I had been baptized in court.

I will never forget the morning I was traveling south on NW 27th Avenue when all of a sudden I heard the loudest explosion, I had ever heard and off to my right I saw a huge fireball shoot into the air. My first reaction to think that somebody had set off a bomb. Knowing the area I then realized that the fireball came from a bottle gas plant just off NW 27th Avenue and the railroad tracks. I headed that direction and while informing the dispatcher to send all available fire units and back up officers I arrived in front of the plant just as three more explosions took place and I saw three bottle gas tank shoot high into the air. I threw my car in reverse and headed backwards down the street as fast as I could go. About this time the fire units began arriving on the scene and started to fight the blaze. It turned out that a delivery driver forgot to unhook a hose as he pulled away from the tank he was filling his truck up from which set off the blaze and started blowing up the small tanks sitting around on the ground. One fireman had to put on a complete suit of fire proof gear and crawl out on the top of this big tank to shut off a valve before the fire could be brought under control. Luckily nobody was injured and only property damage occurred. I think that during my three and a half years in uniform in central district, I help fight as many fires as did some firefighters.

One day about one week before my first Christmas on the force, I was on the day shift at this time, the chief of Patrol & Traffic came to me and handed me a set of car keys and told me to go get him a nice 6 foot Christmas tree and put it in the truck of his vehicle. Like a dummy I guess I held out my hand for some money to pay for the tree. The Chief said to me ", Just go get me the damn tree, you don't have to pay for it". He then told me where to go and said to tell the man, at the tree lot that it was for the Chief and that it had better be a nice one. I never asked again, when I was sent out by a superior officer on a detail of any kind.

I was soon moved off the day shift onto the evening shift (3 to 11 pm) and became a training officer and assigned to ride the paddy wagon for prisoner transport. The main job for the wagon crew when we first went on duty was to make the rounds of all the municipal police stations and pick up any prisoners they were holding, from traffic court in their cities, and take them to the county jail in the courthouse. When we finished, and none of the patrol cars had any prisoners, we were free to patrol the entire district as we saw fit. The regular patrol cars, each had a zone to ride and stay in unless sent some place else as back up.

The funny part about the paddy wagon was that it had no red light nor siren and it looked just like the Hasty Tasty sandwich truck that went around to construction sites selling sandwiches and other things to eat. We called the the roach coaches. More people tried to flag us down and got mad when we did not stop for them. A few times we would stop and offer them rides to the County Jail and they would just laugh and say no thanks.

One evening an officer that was riding the zone of Rickenbacker Causeway and Crandon Park on Key Biscayne. Now this area is isolated and completely surrounded by the City of Miami so I was waiting for the dispatcher to advise the the City Officer would be in route but hearing none, I advised the dispatcher that we were heading to Key Biscayne from Liberty City which was some 12 miles away. Having no red light nor siren I was blowing the horn and flashing the headlights off and on bright while my partner was hanging out the passenger window blowing his whistle and waving a flashlight. I ,still had not heard, what had happened on the Key, but the Officer advised he was okay and had one subject in custody and two others had ran from him. Having just arrived, on the Key in record time and being the first to arrived, I pulled the paddy wagon across the road behind the toll booth to block any cars from getting off Key Biscayne. Soon other cars started arriving and they all wondered how we got there first with out any red light or siren. I told them we put out the wings and flew. It seems that the officer had come upon some teenage boys drinking beer and one jumped him and the other two ran away. The other two were found hiding in some bushes and We ended up their means of transportation off the Key and oh yes they went to the County Jail.

I remember one November day in 1963, November 23rd, to be exact. I was on the way to the station for duty with a fellow officer that lived near me in Carol City, when the Radio Station broke the news that President Kennedy had been shot and killed. My fellow officer and I always took turns driving which made it nice as we lived in North Dade County in Carol City and the new station that had been built was in town just across from the Miami Police Department along the Miami River.

The new station was in fact part of a three building complex which held the new Public Safety Department Headquarters and was attached to the new state of the art County Jail which was then attached to the new Justice Building which contained the Criminal & County Courts and other county facilities.

I remember the day that they opened the new County Jail and we had to transfer all the prisoners from the top floors of the courthouse to the new jail. We formed convoy after convoy of police cars and paddy wagons and it took most of morning to complete the move. It was so nice not to have to drive into the basement of the downtown courthouse and then have to wait on an elevator to take the prisoner though the public up to the jail. The new jail had what is called a sally-port were you signal a guard inside the jail to open the gate and then you drive into an enclosed courtyard. Once inside the courtyard you would wait until the gate was down and locked before you removed the prisoner/prisoners from your vehicle. You then had to check your guns through a bank teller like drawer that came out before he would open the door to the jail and let you inside. The new jail was spacious and I do not know if they ever finished the top two floors of the jail.

Another interesting beat we had to patrol was Venetian Causeway, a toll road that ran from the city of Miami to Miami Beach but not within either city's jurisdiction. It is approximately 3 mile long and goes one one island to another including Star Island where now several Celebrities have homes. The toll was 10 cents each way back in 1960 but today the toll is $1.50 per vehicle. There was at the time I patrolled it on a few occasions, one traffic light in an attempt to keep speeding down to a minimum. If you were assigned to patrol this area especially on midnight shift you might imagine how boring it would be come just riding back and forth without much to do as you could not leave the causeway except for a short time to eat or other personal emergency. I remember one night when I was really really bored. I sat on the side road at the one traffic light and it had a run over that would change the light. So for something to do I would run over the trip and change the light if I heard a car coming to see if they would stop or run the red light. To my surprise very few cars ran the red light and those that did never got tickets.

My other favorite place to patrol was Key Biscayne & Rickenbacker Causeway. It was also very boring, with not much to do, but at least there was a 7/11 store where you could buy something to munch on. Some of the guys, that patrolled the area, use to eat at the Key Biscayne Hotel (on the house too) and like the assignment. One night I stopped a vehicle for doing in excess of 100 miles per hour heading off the causeway. After I had asked the male driver for his license he asked me what I was going to do. I told him I was going to issue him a speeding ticket. He told me in no uncertain terms that I could not do that as he worked at the Key Biscayne Hotel and that they fed us there. I politely informed him that I had never eaten at the Key Biscayne Hotel and probably never would and that I would see him in court. I guess this made some higher-up mad at me and I was never again assigned to patrol Key Biscayne, much to my pleasure. I guess somebody thought they were punishing me. The joke was on them.

I found out if you made somebody's list that had the power to transfer you you would leave patrol & traffic and end up working in the County Jail. This was tried on me a couple of time but I had made some friends that were in charge of running the jail and was told if I wanted to come work for them they would gladly have me but if I did not wish to work there that it would never come to be. I forget exactly when the County Fathers created the Corrections Division and removed the County Jail out of the responsibility of the Public Safety Director/ Metropolitan Sheriff.

During the first two and one half years on the force, if I remember correctly, we went through three different Sheriffs. The position was elective when I first went on then it became appointive then back to elective and then it became appointive once again and E. Wilson Purdy be came the Public Safety Director/Metropolitan Sheriff. During this time of musical chairs I also managed to be sworn in as a Deputy Constable ,so there could not be any questions arise as to whether I had arrest powers. This also gave me a chance to make some extra money by going on trips to return prisoners that had been arrested out of Dade County on warrants issued by the Justice of the Peace's Office. The money came in handy as I was buying a house and was engaged to be married. When I joined the Department I was making $365.00 per month, can you believe that. It was however good and steady money for that time. When I left after 25 years I was making over $36,000 per year and had earned a nice retirement income from the State of Florida. Now I hear that some of the older officer fixing to retire are making $60,000 to $70,000 or more. At least for the twenty three years that I have been retired I have received a cost of living adjustment of 3% which has comes in handy and with my Social Security income for the past eleven years I have been able to make ends meet without having to work unless I really wanted to.

The job did have some embarrassing moments for me and for others. One such moment was during roll call at the old Metro Annex during firearms inspection when an officer drawing his weapon for inspection accidentally (he said) fired his weapon and we all hit the floor.

One time when I had stopped a traffic violator and was forced to arrest him, I was in the process of searching him for weapons with my backside exposed to on coming traffic's view when I heard the sound of my pants ripping and my undies were exposed to all the traffic approaching me on this busy street from the rear. I know they all got a big laugh out of that. I had to call my wife and have her bring me another pair of pants to the County Jail. I guess I had eaten too many donuts lately, or thats what a lot of people think that policemen do all day is drink coffee and eat donuts.

Another moment I remember is when My partner and I got out of our car to guard some prisoners for another unit. I took the shotgun and my partner was using his service revolver. When the task was over and we got back into our vehicle my partner asked me what I would have done, if I would have had to shoot the shotgun. I said "I would just shoot". He said "Like hell you would have, you forgot to load the shotgun".

In our district we had a large warehouse and industrial area to patrol. One day when I had been assigned the big paddy I decided to patrol a warehouse that was getting broken into every now and then. Well you could not see the back of the building because the railroad tracks ran behind the building . So I got the bright idea to go down the tracks to check the back of the building. My partner could not believed that I turned the paddy wagon down the tracks and was able to straddle the tracks. It paid off, as we apprehended four subjects fleeing the loading dock area. The only bad part was my Sergeant happened by and saw the paddy wagon on the tracks unattended. Boy talk about a rear end chewing. He didn't care we caught the bad guys.

I thought I had left Uniform Patrol after I had made Sergeant in 1964, but I once again found myself back in uniform and assigned to a squad of men, when the Republican National Convention hit Miami Beach August 5th through the 8th of 1968. That would prove to be some kind of experience. The hippies had taken over Flamingo Park on Miami Beach and turned it to a big love fest and protest convention. The air on South Beach continuous reeked of Mary Jane (marijuana) and it was not unusual to see a few naked streakers. Because of the size of the gathering and fearing for the safety of the convention my Department was placed on 24 hours duty and when we were not patrolling our regular areas of the county we were sent to guard the Convention Center and to keep out the unwanted crowds. Sometimes working with the National Guard Troops. It was funny because we hardly ran into any Miami Beach Policemen and we often wondered where they were. I did see the Chief of Police one time when he came around to were my men and I were stationed at the rear of the Convention Hall. The hippies were attempting to tear down the fence that had been erected around the Convention Hall. The Chief came up to me and said don't hurt any of them if they tear down the fence. I told him that he was crazy, and that if they tore down the fence my squad would repel them by what ever means we could. We had been loaded down with all kinds of tear gas and mace and I was not going to hesitate to use that force which be necessary to repel them to keep any of my squad from getting hurt. It was some fun and we all were glad that it was over and we went back to our regular duties.

It seems that in my early years on the force when the Sheriff was still elected, that most of the Liquor Store in the district would give out free bottle of booze to any officer that wanted some Christmas Cheer. I was riding with a partner that took a drink now and then but I had to give up an occasional drink after having a Kidney Stone attack. I told my partner that he could have mine if he want it. So we stopped by Goldie's Liquors 42nd Area and went inside. As soon as we got inside the man behind the counter said "The Sergeant and Lieutenant were just here and picked up the bottles for everybody. We said okay and left. When we got up the road, there were the good old Sergeant and Lieutenant parked under a tree dividing up the bottles and putting them in their respective trucks of their squad car. They were so busy they did not even see us go by. About 15 minutes later we heard a holdup go out to another zone car to respond to Goldie's Liquor store. Being close by we went back to out Goldie's, stuck our heads in the door and told them that since every thing was okay, the good old Sergeant and Lieutenant would be there to handle the robbery and we drove off. The robbers were later caught and arrested.

    At one time in Dade County, illegal lotteries seemed to flourish. We were told not to take any action if we came across any such lotteries,as we should just turn it over to the Vice Squad of Detectives. As a matter of fact we were told to call a supervisor to the scene to get his okay before we could make any arrest. This one, supposed, candy store was a big time operator and would write the winning numbers on the bricks in front of the store. Just for the hell of it one day my partner and I decided to stop in the candy store to buy a bar of candy to munch on. When we entered the store we heard a bunch of running and the back went open and 6 or 7 men ran out the back door. I was looking in the candy case on only saw about 3 candy bars in the case and I didn't like any of them. I did notice however along side the candy bars were piles of lottery tickets. We then looked in the back room, from where the men came running, and there were more lottery tickets and about $5,000 in cash. Knowing that my Sergeant was out of service I asked for the Motor Squad Sergeant to come by our location. When the Sergeant arrived I explained what we found and what had happened and I asked what to do about it because of what we had been told. He told us to collect the evidence and arrest the store owner and put him in jail which we did. We filed the charges at the Justice of the Peace Court where a preliminary hearing would be held to see if the case should be bound over to Criminal Court for trial. I appeared in court with the evidence including the

$5,000 . After I testified the Justice of the Peace told me he would take the case and evidence under advisement and would rule later on the charge. I obtained a receipt for the 5 grand and left. I never heard about the case again and I never went back to court on it.

I will never forget the first Aggravated Assault call I was on. We were sent to JMH (Jackson Memorial Hospital) ER. Once there we were taken into a room that had a black male lying on a gurney, on his stomach, and a doctor was in the process of sewing up a 15 inch cut across the right-side of his back. I got his name and other information I needed for my report and then I asked him if he knew who cut him. He said of course he knew who it was it was his friend girl. I asked if he wanted to press charges against her . He replied "Well I guess I ought to as this is the third time she has cut me and she has also shot me twice" but I love her too much to press charges. She was just mad cause she caught me with another girl. Oh did I mention the fact that shortly after we arrived at the ER and after seeing all the blood and wound, I found myself sitting in a chair with somebody pushing down on the back of my neck that was between my legs shouting for me to sit up. I yelled that I would sit up if whoever it was would take their hands off the back of my neck. After I sat up I asked what the hell happened? I was told that I fainted. That was the first and only time that the sight of blood ever bothered me.

When I first came on the department there wasn't any County run ambulance services. The ambulance services were left up to two or three private ambulance companies or any funeral home that want to serve as an ambulance and receive payment from the county if the patient could not pay. Needless to say this resulted into chaos sometimes at a scene of an accident with injuries. Several times I was sent to handle an accident only to arrive and find two different funeral homes almost coming to blows over who was going to haul the patient. This all changed when Randall Eastern became the

County's Ambulance service and was dispatched via our dispatchers.

Speaking of Dispatchers, we had this one dispatcher who could not pronounce "3". It would always seems to come out as tree. I could not believe it when one early morning I came across an abandon vehicle at N. W. 33 Avenue and N. W. 33 Street and it was unbelievable but the tag on the vehicle was "33W33. When I requested a check on the tag number all I heard for about 3 minutes was dead silence. I than asked if she read the license and when she keyed her mike all I heard in the background was a bunch of other dispatchers laughing like crazy. Finally she composed herself and this is what she said "Tag tree tree W tree tree is QRU" and then silence, so I replied QSL thank you tree.

I had been on the force one and half years when I met my future wife, one day when myself and buddy I had grown up with, were eating at a Huddle House restaurant in North Miami. This was in September of 1961 and we got engaged on Christmas eve and married July 28, 1962.

I wanted to do something special for the coming New year so My buddy and I and my wife decided to to throw a New Year's Eve party. We rented a hall, hired a band and invited all of my squad I worked with and all our friends. We danced the night sway and really had a great time. Oh yes, we used designated drivers too.

January 1964 was a very pleasant time as I found out that my wife, Chiquita Faye was pregnant with my son who was then born on September 13, 1964. I thought he was going to be born sooner, like in August, as Hurricane Cleo popped up in a hurry and my wife was admitted to North Shore hospital because of the storm.

Low pressure usually brings on deliveries of babies for some reason. The storm came and went with no birth until the next month. My wife was in the hospital and I was working 12 hour shifts because of the storm. If you have never driven around in a hurricane you have never had so much fun. I was home one night during the storm, after working a twelve hour shift sweeping the water out the sliding glass doors that had blown in around the front door of my house. I had placed plywood over all the windows and water was also coming in the windows on the north-side of the house somehow. The front door was shaking so bad I thought it was going to blow down the door that I got big spikes and drove them through the door into the door jab in hopes that it would hold the door in place. It worked.

Then all of a sudden the phone rang and I thought surely it would be the hospital telling me my son had been born but instead it was parents in Dayton, Ohio calling to see if we were okay. I asked how in the world did you get through we are just now in the eye of the storm. I informed them that we were fine and that as a precaution Chickie (Chiquita), my wife was in the hospital. The storm blew over and the sun came out. I was lucky, that my home had no carpet, and had all terrazzo floors hence the water did little damage.

We were still having the back part of Hurricane Cleo when I went to work the next day. I was still riding the paddy wagon and I could not believe that I was requested to the prison ward at JMH (Jackson Memorial Hospital) and told to transfer some prisoners to the county jail which at this time was still in the downtown courthouse. I was sure glad that nothing happened to any of the prisoners that I was told to take out into the storm instead of waiting until the storm had completely cleared. It makes you wonder what goes through the minds of those in charge.

We use to make frequent round ups on Northwest 18th Avenue in Liberty City and roust all the drunks and tell them to go home or if necessary we would put them in jail over night for safe keeping. One such night while we were making the rounds a certain

Lieutenant arrived on the scene and instead of letting us send them on the way to their homes, He started ordering us to put them all in jail and called for the patty wagon to come and pick them all up. He said with a proud voice, This will teach them to go home and sleep it off.

   Well sometimes even if it was just for Public Drunkenness you would have to appear in court to testify. Well this meant getting up in the morning and going all the way to court and not getting extra pay but what was called court time which could be taken off at some later time. So we all came up with a plan and we all signed the Lieutenants name to all the arrests forms before putting them in the paddy wagon and sending them off to jail. Boy was he mad when he had to go to court. I would never and never did sign my name to an arrest report on somebody that I was told to arrest. A couple of other times this happen and I just told them if they wanted the person arrested for them to sign the arrest report.

   I remember the first time I had to appear in Judge Ben Willard's Court. I had arrested a man in Liberty City for breaking into and apartment in the housing project. I had received the call as a burglary in progress. As I was arriving on the scene and my back up nowhere in site I was met by a man with a cast on his arm, he showed me the apartment, and told me they were still inside. As I cautiously approached the apartment a man was exiting the rear door carrying a small TV and a small radio. I placed him under arrest and put him in the back set of my patrol car and had him handcuffed to the seat belt. I asked the man with the cast on his hand to yell if he tried to get away. I went back to the apartment and was fixing to enter, when I heard a loud scream coming from my patrol car. I, ran back, thinking the man with the cast had been hurt. To my surprise it was the other way around. The man I had arrest was bleeding from his forehead. I asked the man with the cast what had happened and he told me the man tried to get out of the car and I told him to stop but when he didn't I hit him with my cast. As it turned out he was the only burglar upon searching the apartment when my backup arrived. When this case came to court the burglar, when asked about the wound on his forehead would only say he hit me, he hit me. The Judge then asked "you mean to say this officer hit you". No Sir he answered the other guy hit me when I tried to get out of the police car. I then explained about the man with the cast on his arm. The Judge gave him two years in the county jail. Sometimes while on patrol you have to improvise and come up with all kinds of things to get the job done.

One night on the midnight shift a car in the zone next to my partner and I, was dispatched to a burglary alarm ringing at a Liquor Store. We were dispatched as a two man unit for back up. As we pulled up we heard the other office yell "I told you to put your hands up that we had you surrounded". The first officer on the scene had been running from corner to corner of the building yelling in different voices to make believe he was not alone. If I remember right he even fired a warning shot when one looked over the edge to make him stay away from the edge. We called for the fire department to respond with their ladder truck so we could get up to the roof and arrest the subject. They had been working on cutting a hole through the roof so they could get inside. They did not know that in doing so they had set off the silent alarm.

There was never a really dull day on the force. You always seem to stay busy answering domestic calls or writing accident reports or responding to burglaries. I was dispatched to a burglary call one day and as I approached a kid came running out the back door and took off running across some back yards. I took off after him but he seemed to be getting away so I decided to fire a warning shot. So I yelled halt or I will shoot and then fired a shot into the ground. The boy stopped in his tracks which was great as he was approaching a fence and I knew if he jumped I, and made it, he would have been gone. I asked for GIU detectives to respond the the scene and when they arrived I turned him over to them. Later I was asked by the two detectives what I had done to the boy. I asked what they were talking about. They told me that on the way to the station they started smelling something and asked the boy if he had stepped in dog poop while he was running and he said "No I messed my pants". They told me he then said" What, would you have done with a cop chasing you and shooting at you. I told them I had fired a warning shot into the ground and it worked. The boy told the detectives that he was going stop because the 50 silver dollars in his pants, that he had stolen were pulling his pants down and making it hard for him to run.

Another task that you would some times be honored with was called the mail run. This would entail going from the headquarters building down to the south end of the county to the Perrine Station (#4) and pick up all interoffice mail going to Headquarters and deliver the mail from Headquarters to them. Then you traveled to the Miami International Airport Station (#3) and pick up their mail and deliver their mail. From there it was off to Carol City Station (#1) to the north and continued the routine. Then it was back to Headquarters (#2) and deliver the mail. I felt like an express mailman. At least if took your time you could use up most of the day. It was a good way to learn about the other three District Stations at this time. Later Stations 5, 6, & 7 would be built and established for better coverage.

I remember one time while riding the paddy wagon we were sent to the Airport to transport a prisoner to the County Jail. When we arrived at the Airport I asked if the prisoner had been searched, and was informed that he had been searched, and that he had nothing on his person. As my usual routine I began another search of the prisoner. I could not believe what I found. The man had $5,000.00 in cash in his pockets. I said "I thought you guys had searched him", then why did I find all this cash on him. I filled out a property receipt for the money and had the subject sign it that it was taken off him and then the officer I was taking the prisoner from signed then I signed. Upon leaving I advised the dispatcher that I was in route to the County Jail with a prisoner and his $5,000.00 cash. I would have caught holy hell if I had not found it and they did at the jail. The prisoner could have easily have said he had $10,000.00 and I took $5,000.00. I made sure they signed for the money at the jail.

This taught me a lesson never to take somebodies word that they had searched a prisoner. Having been regularly assigned to ride as Car 650 (the paddy wagon) I usually was assigned new officers to act as their training or breaking in officers. I guess I did a good job, or else I was being punished, being assigned this task. One of my new trainees, Fred Taylor, even went on to become the Director (Sheriff) of the Department. One thing I always remember about him is that he liked strawberry milkshakes. We would stop and get one at Burger King the first thing out of the station. He would always take the lid off his and somehow the squad car would sooner or later lurch causing him to have strawberry shake on his tie. You did good Fred (oops).

A lot of eating places would give officers on duty in uniform a discount on their meals when they ate. I found out that they figured it was good insurance to have a Uniformed Police Car sitting at their place of business to give a hit to any trouble makers or thieves that the police might show up at any time. I always made it a practice to hand the person running the restaurant the total amount of the bill and if I got back change and a break that was great. I remember one Sergeant would run by this particular Burger King when he got off work and take home a bag of food for the evening meal. Well after a few times Burger King got fed up and stopped giving half price or even free coffee to officers. Some people new how to spoil a good thing.

It just so happened that next door to this Burger King was a Food Fair Grocery Store. One day after having some coffee as my partner and I were leaving, a car went speeding out of the Food Fair parking lot and somebody was standing in the front door yelling they just robbed me. Well needless to say we gave chase. As we were flying across N. W. 79 Street behind the fleeing vehicle, we began to be pelted with packages of meat. After we were able to finally pull the subjects over and arrest them, we had to go back and retrieve all the packages of meat. Most of them were steaks of all kinds that they had shoplifted from the Food Fair Store.

   I remember the time that myself and Officer Paul Anderson was assigned to go with the Vice Squad when they raided a pool hall on Northwest 27th Avenue. I was asked to go inside with the officers who were in plain clothes. The sent Officer Anderson around to the back door before we entered the building and told him to make sure that nobody got out the back door. Well when we hit the back room where all the gambling was going on the tables went flying with money and chips flying all over the place. Five of the subjects that had been playing in the games hit the back door running almost tearing it off the hinges. Well, when we went outside we expected to see one or two in custody but all five subjects were lying on the ground with their hands on their head.

   Officer Anderson it seems had found a two by four on the way around back and took it with him. When they came out the back door he floored them all with one swing of the two by four. The Vice Squad took them all in for illegal gambling, even though nobody would own up to all the cash lying on the table. It didn't hurt the fact that Officer Anderson was a big man and weighed about 250 lbs. I also remember the time that Officer Anderson responded to an alarm going off in a pay telephone booth. Southern Bell was having a plague of pay telephones being robbed by somebody shooting out the lock on the coin box with a 22 caliber rifle. Well when Officer Anderson arrived on the scene he was in such a hurry to get out of his squad car he didn't get the vehicle stopped before the phone booth and he hit it knocking it over trapping the subject inside. We all kidded him about the fact that Southern Bell was paying $50.00 for the arrest and conviction of anyone robbing a pay phone and he wanted to make sure he had an air tight case. Officer Anderson was in the Police Academy with me. Sad to say but Officer Anderson was killed shortly after this incident in a vehicle accident while he was responding to and emergency call.

During the Police Academy we were given a tour of the South Florida Mental Hospital in South Broward County to acquaint us with the care given to persons with mental problems. When we entered on ward a man started screaming, I Know you, I know you and he ran up to Officer Paul Anderson. He said you were Santa Claus in our High School play. It is funny how you run into people you know in the oddest places.

I remember another sad day when I was asked to go check on another officer that was with me in the Police Academy, as he had not showed up for work. When I arrived at his home I received no answer to my knocks but I could hear a radio playing in the house. When I went around to the back door and looked through the window in the kitchen door I saw him lying on the floor in full uniform and a coffee cup on the floor beside him. I kicked open the door and determined that he was dead. A search of the house revealed his wife and unborn child and his mother-in-law and dead. I then realized that there was a strong odor of gas in the house and I was forced to leave the house. It was later learned that all of them had been overcome with gas and died not knowing what was even going on. One never knows when it is they time to go.

As I started my career with the Police Department I also embarked on another career at the same time. A friend of mine asked me if the County Fraternal Order of Police Lodge would sponsor a youth baseball team in West North Miami as they were short on team sponsor for the up coming season. Being a new member of the Fraternal Order of Police Metro Dade Lodge #6, I told my friend that I would ask and the next meeting which was the following week. Boy did I ever put my foot in it. When I asked the President of the Lodge Charlie Maddox, he said sure we will, if you manage the team. I found out that they would only sponsor teams coached by Police Officer, for the Public Relations aspect, having Police Officers being friendly and working with kids. I told Charlie Maddox that I would need $350.00 for equipment and uniforms. Charlie then told me to go see the man standing near the podium and ask him for a donation and be sure and tell him it was for the kids. Well I approached the man and I introduced myself and advised him that I had just become the new manager of a youth baseball team in North Miami and needed to raise $350.00 for equipment and uniforms. I was surprised when he reached into his pocket and came out with a fifty dollar bill. I thank him very much and went back to see Charlie Maddox. Charlie asked me how much I got from Sammy Spears and I almost fell over when I found out who he was. Sammy Spears was the band leader for the Jackie Gleason Show.

   I then asked Charlie how can I get the rest of the money I needed and he told me come see him tomorrow and he would have an answer for me. When I went to see Charlie the next day he handed me a stack of raffle tickets for a bunch of prizes and told me to sell them and keep the money for the team. Well I managed to raised another $290.00 for the team so off I went to get the equipment and uniforms. I found some blue pants trimmed in gold and some pullover gold shirts trimmed in blue. I asked Charlie what I should put on the uniforms and he told me FRATERNAL ORDER OF POLICE METRO DADE LODGE # 6. I told him he must be dreaming as that would not fit on an adult shirt let alone a 13 or 14 year old shirt. I settled for F O P #6. So the first season all the other teams called us the FOPS. We had a great first year even if we only won 1 game and that was against the team that won the championship. Many more years coaching followed and year I coached I would take the boys out on a Charter Boat called the Capt. RUDY docked at Haulover Marina. The Captain was an auxiliary member of the Police Lodge. My career with Little League Baseball ended when I retired from the Department in 1985. I was so proud of all on my kids I had coached over the years, as not one that I know of ever got in trouble with the law.

On November 7, 1962 a gold coin bracelet along with other jewelry were stolen in a burglary. No arrests were ever made to date. On January 11, 1964 the bracelet in question was seen on the wrist of the wife of the Chief of Detectives at a local race track. The sheriff was notified and made an inquiry as to the circumstances surrounding possession of the bracelet. The Chief of Detectives informed the Sheriff that the bracelet was given to his wife by an attorney who specializes in criminal law. The attorney stated he had been given the bracelet by a client who owned a notorious bistro. This was confirmed by the nightclub owner who stated he had found the bracelet in his nightclub and when no one claimed it, he had given it as a gift to his attorney. A positive identification of the bracelet was made by the true owner. The Sheriff's Office investigation of the witnesses was completed. No formal statement was taken from the attorney or his client, or the operator of the nightclub. The investigating officers permitted a statement to be prepared by the attorney and client and delivered to the Sheriff's Office the following day. At no time did anyone question the Chief of Detectives' wife, nor was any statement taken from her. The Grand Jury did not speculate as to what evidence might have been obtained had a more prompt and efficient investigation, free of irregularities, been conducted immediately. Surely, the Grand Jury stated that, the public has a right to expect a thorough and complete investigation, by proper authorities, when a high ranking police official's wife is in the possession of stolen property. After hearing the testimony of all the parties involved, the Grand Jury found insufficient evidence to warrant criminal charges. The Grand Jury however was dissatisfied with the manner in which the Sheriff's Office had investigated this matter when it was brought to their attention.

One of the things you would run into from time to time especially in the projects, were a lot of people lived in a small confined area, was child birth calls. I shall never forget the first call of that nature that I received. I was dispatched to a woman in labor with Randall Eastern ambulance on the way. Upon my arrival I knocked on the door, and Identified myself, and right away a lady came to the door. I asked where the lady was that was in labor to which she politely informed me that it was her. I was trying to get her over to the couch in the living room. To my surprise on the way to the couch she yelled out here it comes and as she went to the floor the baby appeared and was born. I thought sure it was hurt but it seemed fine so I picked up the baby boy and gave him to his mother on the couch. I ask her if she had any other children and she said "Lordy yes this in my 12th" . I said it is no wonder that she had no trouble with her labor and why it was over so fast.

Randall Eastern arrived and checked over the mother and baby boy and stated they were both fine and took them to Jackson Memorial Hospital. She asked me what my first name was when she was leaving and I told her Robert and asked why she want to know. She told me that I had just helped deliver Robert. I was on several calls when the ambulance crew would be in a hurry to get the mother into the ambulance and to the hospital so that they would not have to deliver the baby in their ambulance and have to clean up the mess. I had one other baby named after me during my time in the projects and her name was Roberta.

While riding the Liberty City area, I had a road Sergeant Ray "B" who was a very articular person. On every report and ticket you wrote, he wanted all the "I" dotted and all the "T" crossed and no erasures or white out. He once made me sit and write an accident report over four times before he would accept it. He came out on the road from the County Jail on top of the downtown courthouse for which the county jail took up the top three floors. Having worked the paddy wagon a long time, I had already met him at the jail. He even wanted me to correct somebody's arrest report. I told him no way was I altering an official report and that he could do it if he wanted to. I guess he remembered me when he came out on the road. Sgt. Ray "B" later went on and became a Homicide Investigator and was a really good one as he left no leaf unturned. I was working in General Investigations Unit North District when I ran into him again. The Homicide Unit was overloaded one day and I and another Detective was sent out to handle a shooting which resulted in a death. Well we had cleaned the case all up and had arrested the subject when along came Sgt. Ray "B" and told us he would take over the case. I said okay but there is nothing left to do. We had already taken him before a Justice of the Peace. In fact I had to type up the warrant and charges for the Justice as it was the weekend and his Secretary was off. So I handed him my report and asked him to drop it off at Homicide when he went to the office.

I set a record one evening driving the paddy wagon when the Vice Squad made a raid on a night club that was a front for prostitution. I hauled forty three prisoners to the County Jail in the courthouse and upon entering the basement drive the paddy wagon got hung up on the rear platform which caused the back wheels to be lifted off the pavement. We had to unload and the ladies of the evening and a few gents before I could drive the rest of the way into the basement. This entailed having some jailers come down from the jail to take the prisoners onto the elevators, to take them up to the jail. I made sure from then on, not to over load the paddy wagon.

Well, in November, 1964 they finally started promoting from the Sergeant's list that I was on. They had promoted five officers to Sergeant when the list first came out, I believe in May of 1964. We were beginning to wonder if anyone else would be promoted before the list expired at the end of the year. Well the good news came and I was promoted to Sergeant and was assigned to the Central District G. I. U. (General Investigations Unit). So the next morning, I arrived bright and early, as I had no idea as to what I was going to be doing. I had worked from time to time with some detectives and I really did not know what happen to a case once I had written my report turned things over to them, and now here I AM ONE. The Administrative Sergeant, Bill Wright, gave me a briefcase and a set of guidelines to read. The Sergeant, all of a sudden after he hung the phone, threw me a set of car keys and told me that they had a dead body and that Homicide did not have anyone that could respond, so I was assigned the case to respond and check out the scene. Upon my arrival at the scene there was an older man lying on the floor. The ambulance crew was still on the scene and advised me that the man was dead and there did not appear to be any wounds. I told them that they could go and I requested requested that the ME Office (Medical Examiner) send a unit to pick up the body and I left and went back to the office. When I walked into the office Sgt. Wright asked me what the hell I did with the ME report. I told him, I did not know anything about any ME report. He then kindly explained to me that I was supposed to fill out an ME report containing the Victim's information, next of kin if known and signs of a homicide.

So off I went to the ME's Office to fill out said report. The ME also likes to know if the victim has past health problems or any conditions on the scene that might cause the death. So much for my case as an investigator in GIU. The rest of the day was spent being trained on how to handle various scenes and when to refer cases to other specialized units such as Robbery, Homicide, Auto Theft, Vice Squad or Sex Crimes. The next day I was assigned a partner and we went out to investigate some blood found in a motel room. When we arrived, the bed in the room was covered with blood. We also found an instrument used in those days for performing abortions. My partner and I gathered all the information and facts that we had obtained and wrote our report and referred the case to the Homicide Unit.

When left the motel we were assigned a case of stolen orchid plants. We worked on this case for the next several days. I sure learned a lot about flowers and orchids in particular. Each orchid plant has it own characteristics much like human fingerprints. They can be positively identified by these characteristics. We received a few tips and found the orchids or most of them at least at a flower show the following week. This made the owner very happy as he considered them like they were his children. Some of the orchids only bloom once every 7 years. The thief was convicted in court and sent to Raidford Prison for a 15 years sentence, on a conviction of Grand Larceny charge.

I quickly picked up on the in and out of investigation and interrogation and was able to function on my own. While some of the officers assigned to GIU were patrolmen if they were the lead investigator and you were assigned to assist them on a case, you in effect had a sergeant working for a patrolman.

I remember the first interrogation that I sat in on. I was given a telephone book, and told to sit in a chair by the light switch. I was told that when I was told to do so, I was to turn off the lights and drop the telephone book on the floor so it would make a loud noise. I did as I was asked to do and when I turned the lights back on, the two Detectives doing the interrogation asked me if I saw or heard anything. How could I the lights were off and all I heard was the phone book hitting the floor. They then asked the subject if he was ready to confess and write out a statement or did he want the other Detective to turn off the lights again. He said that he was willing to write out a statement. I was left only to guess what happen while the lights were out.

I had only been working at Central GIU for a few months when I was called into the Lieutenant's office. Lieutenant Sandstrom went on to explain that he had to transfer an investigator to the North District GIU, in Carol City, and since I was the newest Detective, guess who was chosen to go. He did not know it but I was saying thank you, thank you, under my breath. I told him that it was alright and that I didn't mind the transfer. I just told him I was glad that I was not going back into uniform. I was happy I lived only 23 blocks from that station, which was located at Northwest 37th Avenue and the Palmetto Expressway.

The Public Safety Department shared this station with a Metro Fire Department Unit. The station was divided into two parts, one being for the Police Uniform and GIU units and the other half was for the firefighters. It would take some getting use too after having so much room in the Central District Headquarters Building along with all the specialized units. North District was located in a little shopping center which also housed a Super Market, Restaurant and a few other small shops, which made it nice for shopping and lunch.

The GIU at this station handled all General Investigations from NW 95th Street on the south to the Broward County Line on the north and from the Atlantic Ocean on the east to the Collier County line on the west. I was amazed at the number of cases that came in during a weeks time. Each investigator was assigned between 7 and 10 new cases per week. On each case we would have 10 days to make a preliminary investigation and write some kind of report. We would mark the case, open pending further information (which meant we had no leads), closed by arrest (meant you made an arrest in the case) or Exceptionally Cleared (meant you found out who committed the crime but no charges would be filed in the case for one reason or another) or last it would be marked Unfounded (meant the crime never happened).

   We had two large Country Clubs in our District, with some prestigious people living there. Ones was Called Miami Lakes Country Club and the other was called The Country Club of Miami. One such person was Senator Robert Graham who owned most of what was Carol City. Senator Graham went on to be Governor of Florida and then a United States Senator. His family once had a huge dairy farm and lots of cattle that roamed the area. Senator Graham also built a new community called Miami Lakes. Senator Graham lived in the Miami Lakes Community and in The Country Club of Miami lived the Famous Jackie Gleason. In order to attract Jackie Gleason to the Country Club Of Miami the built him a home right on the edge of the golf course along with a separate building which was Jackie's private poolroom. They also built him a large office building at the entrance to the country club from which he ran his show (The Jackie Gleason Show) which was on TV for many years and was filmed and televised from the Miami Beach Convention Center.

   I remember three things that happened that I was called on to investigate and assist on other investigations. The first being that our department had received in formation that there was a plot to a to assassinate Jackie at his next taping of his show on Miami Beach. My Lieutenant and six more of us were assigned the case. We had no idea who the person responsible for the threats, but we took them seriously. Low and behold a man came through the doors without a ticket and acting suspiciously and nervous. He was apprehended by Lieutenant Spath and another detective and he was found to have bomb which he was planning on using if he made it to the stage. Needles to say he was arrested and taken off to jail. The bomb squad came and removed the bomb and disposed of it without harm to anyone. I learned later what a real nice guy Jackie was. When Lieutenant Spath talked to Jackie and told him about what about happened, and was prevented, Jackie didn't even seem to care that his life had just been saved. Lieutenant Spath asked Jackie for a couple of tickets to the next show for his wife and kid and Jackie told him he could buy them just like anybody else. Boy what a nice guy!

   The second time I came into contact with the man named Jackie was when I was asked to investigate a larceny call at the Country Club of Miami club house. Upon arrival at the Country Club of Miami I was directed to the locker room were I once again met the man called Jackie. I could tell that he had been drinking while he was informing myself that a cigarette lighter which had been given to him by Red Skelton had been stolen by a waiter in the restaurant/bar. I asked if he could identify the waiter and he replied in no uncertain terms that the waiters name was Requis. He then stated that he was going to his house a short distance away and that I could reach him there when I got the lighter back. I then went upstairs to the restaurant/bar in search of the waiter named Requis. I was informed by the manager that nobody by that name worked there. I informed the manager that Mr. Jackie told me that he left his cigarette lighter on his table when he got up to leave. He said that the waiter named Requis was cleaning off his table. Jackie said he went out to light a cigarette and when he returned the lighter was gone so Requis had to have taken it. I asked if they had anybody working there with a name that sounded like Requis? They could only come up with one waiter who was working and that was a man name Jose Rodriguez. I talked with Jose and was assured by him that there was no lighter on the table when he cleaned off the table. He allowed me to search his person as well as his locker and no lighter was found. I then proceeded to Mr. Jackie's home and rang the doorbell time after time until he finally opened the door. He asked me what I wanted as he was tired and wanted to go back to bed. I told him that I was there about the lighter he reported stolen. "Oh never mind that" he said, I found the lighter when I got home. It was in my pants pocket. He told he to have a nice day and slammed the door shut. You can probably guess about how happy I was at this point. I had spent almost an hour working the unfounded case and trying to find this Requis fellow that supposedly stole his lighter and he didn't even have enough courtesy or good sense of mind to have called the restaurant and tell then he had found his precious lighter. My second good impression of Mr. Jackie.

The third time that it was my misfortune to have come in contact with Mr. Jackie was when his home was broken into. I responded to investigate and obtain a list of missing items and to search for other clues. Mr Jackie was not at home and I was met by his housekeeper. She told me that Jackie and Honey Merrill, his personal assistant, were on a cruise and would not be back for two weeks. I requested a mobile crime lab respond and process the scene for fingerprints and process the scene for other possible evidence. The point of entry into the house was via a bathroom window, which by chance was the only window in the house not protected by the burglar alarm system. The house keeper was hesitant to allow the crime lab tech to process the scene, but I assured her, this was the only way we might solve the crime.

There were found some latent marks indicating that whom ever broke into the home knew, two things. One, was that the window was not alarmed and two, that he would not leave fingerprints as he had socks on his hands. The one thing the burglar forgot was that he would leave footprints with no socks on his bare feet. Several footprints were found on the tile floor under the window that was entered. I was reasonably certain that whom ever broke in knew Mr. Jackie, and knew the layout of the house and knew that this particular window was not alarmed. Since not much was taken in the burglary, I also suspected a juvenile. One person that fit this assumption and profile was a son of Mr. Jackie's personal assistant Honey Merrill.

   Upon interviewing him, I asked if I could take his prints to compare then against the ones found at the crime scene and he said "sure" go ahead I have nothing to hide. He must have been thinking about fingerprints, but when I asked him to take off his shoes his mouth dropped wide open. He knew I then had him and sure enough his footprints matched those found at the crime scene. He told me that he broke into the house to get back at Mr. Jackie for the way he treated his mother. Of course Mr. Jackie did not want to press charges against the lad, but I explained that it was up to the Juvenile Court System if charges would be file. I later found out through a grapevine that Mr. Jackie made a $10,000.00 donation to a South Dade Catholic Boys School/Home like that of Father Flanagan's Boys Town in Nebraska. That was the last I ever heard of about case and Mr. Jackie. It wasn't too much longer that his shows were over on Miami Beach and he moved from the Country Club of Miami. Goodbye Mr. Jackie.

   In the 36 years that I lived in Miami, I went through a lot of Hurricanes. I remember Hurricane Betsy in 1965 that did a lot of damage especially to the Saxony Hotel at 3201 Collins Avenue on Miami Beach. Well, it seems like a group of five high school students while wandering on the beach found a way into the boarded up hotel still undergoing repairs from Betsy. They had a time in the next few days removing most of the TV sets from the hotel. As it turned out two detectives and myself had been working a gang of guys who had been breaking into a bunch of GM cars for radios and anything else they could fine of value. We had received information from a source that led us to try and keep our eyes out for them. They had been breaking into schools and cars for some time according to the information supplied to us.

They were soon joined by two older youths one 18 and the other 20. This gave the gang more range as they now had transportation supplied by the older youths stolen off of car lots. They were now able to get off the main land and travel to the Miami Beach area. We finally got a break in the case when they started selling a bunch of TV sets for $40.00 a piece that they had stolen from the Saxony Hotel. A surveillance was placed on the subjects and soon we caught them selling a stolen TV set. This led to the closure of close to fifty Burglaries and Auto Thefts committed by these subjects. The two adults were booked into the County Jail and the three Juveniles were referred into Juvenile Court. It turned out that the two adults had Juvenile records for the same offenses.

My main area for investigations, at this time, turn out to be an area bounded by, South Biscayne River Drive on the North, Northwest 119th Street on the South, Interstate I-95 on the East and Northwest 27th Avenue on the West. I was assigned most of the cases that occurred in this area. It was more or less my beat. As uniform cars have beats to patrol.

I had two main Junior high School in this area. One being Thomas Jefferson Junior High and the other one being Westview Junior High School. I mention these that since most of the Petty Burglaries and small thefts in this area could almost always be traced back to some Juvenile Offender who probably attended one of the two schools. I would make it a practice everyday, when possible, to stop by each school and pick up an absentee list from each school from the Assistant Principals for boys. These lists would give me some possible suspects and very often paid off well.

When I first became a Detective, Truancy was a Delinquency Offense for which a Juvenile could be picked up and referred into Juvenile Court for a hearing. Then in somebody's wisdom it became a Social Offense and you could only pick up a Juvenile and return him or her to the school they belonged in. This took away some leverage we had in fighting crimes being committed by Juveniles.

   The Assistant Principal at Thomas Jefferson Junior High, Mr. "B" would often ride with me when I was looking for a particular Truant so that I could return them to school. Mr. "B" knew them all by sight. We would return them to school or find out why he was absent from school and if the parents knew they were not in school. Mr. "B" would go knock on the front door and I would be standing at the back door waiting for them to run out the back. This worked like a charm most of the time. We would then return them to school, if the parents did not know there were out of school, and then call the parents. I would always ask them to write out a statement to the fact that they had not committed any crimes while they should have been in school and were not. I doing so most of them would unknowingly leave their fingerprints all over the paper they were writing on. I would then take these papers to the Crime Lab, (not todays CSI but close), and have the papers chemically treated which would then produce the Juveniles prints that could be compared against fingerprints found at open case scenes. This paid off many many times.

   One time I remember that while I was talking to this one boy. I told him I thou8ght he was lying, (I was almost sure of it), and as I was leaving I told him to always carry a toothbrush around with him in his back pocket because, when I could prove it, I would come back and put him into Youth Hall (Juvenile Detention), just for lying to me. I was able to match his prints as having been involved I several burglaries and when he walked into the Assistant Principals office, all he said was Mr. Palmer I don't have my toothbrush and he started confessing to everything that he had been involved in. Yes, I kept my promise, which is always important when working with Juveniles, and took and booked him into Youth hall. I know you might say this was illegal but at this time the law did not require him to have a parent or guardian present with him. It only required that I had to advise him that he didn't have to say anything and if he did it could be used against him and to also notify his parents where he would be.

This worked on another case and the boy also handed up the person with whom he had committed several burglaries. The one he handed up turn out to be an adult with whom he had gotten mad at. When the adult case went to trial and the bot testified in Criminal Court, a funny thing happened. When the Assistant State Attorney rested the State's case against the adult, his attorney move for a Directed Verdict of Acquittal on the grounds that his client was in the City of Hialeah Jail on the day this crime occurred. I was ordered my the Judge to go and immediately call Hialeah Police Department and find out if the subject was in deed in their jail on the day in question. It turn out to be true and the adult was found not guilty. Needless to say my Juvenile witness could not testify in any of the other cases having lied in a Court of Law (committed perjury). The Juvenile had in fact committed 14 other burglaries with the adult subject but as fate would have it the one we went to trial on first we lost and all the others because of his having lied. This first case the Juvenile committed with another Juvenile buddy whom he did not want to get into trouble so he blamed this case on the adult. You win some and you lose some.

There was a time when a boy had been seen at Thomas Jefferson Junior High playing with a stop watch in the classroom, that had been stolen in a Burglary at Biscayne Gardens Elementary School which is just on the other side of the Athletic fields used by both schools. The boy was in Mr. "B"'s office when I arrived. I talked with Mr. "B" before we went in to talk to the boy, to find out what was going on. We both thought he might have found the watch on the Athletic Fields having been dropped there by the burglar in his get away. We then went in the office on the assumption that this boy had stolen the watch. I knew this boy as he had been in some minor trouble before. I just kept asking him when and why he had stolen the watch and why he was dumb enough to bring it to school and play with it in class. He just kept saying Mr. Palmer I did not steal the watch I found it honest. This went on for 20 minutes or so and I finally said I believe you ,take me to the place you found the watch and he said okay. We started out to the Athletic Fields and he said no, you will have to take me in your police car. This took me by surprise.

So into the police car we went, The Boy, Mr. "B" and I. The boy led us directly to a house on North Biscayne River Drive. The boy then said that there was a fort in the back yard with all kinds of stuff in it. He said this is where I found it and took it. He said he figured it was stolen but that who ever put it there would not miss it nor tell on him if they found out he took the watch. He knew the bot that lived there. I went to the front door and knocked and when a lady came to the door I identified myself with my badge and ID card. I told they lady that answered the door that the boy I had in my car brought me here and told me he had stolen a watch out of the fort in her back yard. She informed me that her son and his buddy built the fort and used it to play in, but she had never been inside the fort. I asked her for permission in the presence of Mr. "B" to search the fort, and she said by all means. She went with us and when we got the door to the fort open you would not believe what we found inside. It looked like a drug store with all kinds of candy and stuff and some other items that had been stolen during the Burglary at Biscayne gardens Elementary School.

As it turned out the boy that lived here went to North Miami Senior High School and his buddy lived right across the street from Biscayne Gardens Elementary School were the watch had been stolen from. I impounded all the property in the fort as evidence, gave the lady of the house a receipt which she signed showing that she gave me permission to remove the property from her property, probably not realizing at the time that I would probably be back some time later to pick up her son.

I went through all the property recovered and checked it against lists of property stolen from various places that had been burglarized over a period of six or seven months. Part of the property recovered were a bunch of smoking pipes. These had been taken in a Burglary of a Smoke and Pipe repair shop on Northwest 7th Avenue and Northwest 151st Street. The man that owned the shop was sure glad to hear I had recovered some of his stolen property. He really just wanted to hear that I had recovered one pipe in particular that was irreplaceable and worth approximately $3,000.00. He almost cried with joy when I handed him the pipe. I had luckily brought it with me for him to identify. He identified the pipe and I took a picture of him holding the pipe and left it with him.

I can imagine what was going through the boy's mind, who owned the fort, after I had recovered all the stolen property from his fort and I had not contacted him for almost two weeks. I decided to make him wait and go talk to his buddy first, the one that lived across the street from Biscayne Gardens Elementary School. When I interviewed this boy he confessed to all the burglaries I asked him about and also handed up his partner, the boy that owned the fort. He wrote out a written statement confessing to all his crimes and signed it and the his mother signed it as a witness. I informed the mother that I would have to put her son in Youth Hall until I could talk to the boy involved and his parents. They would release her son into her custody until the Juvenile Court hearing.

Well the interview with the other boy and his parents was not going well. He would not admit to anything and kept saying that he did not know who had put all that stuff in his fort. I got fed up with all his lying and took a chance. I said tell your Mom and Dad how you almost got shot the night you broke into the Drug Store on Northeast 6th Avenue and Northeast 149th Street. Tell them how a police officer came upon the two of you coming out of the store, yelled for you to stop or he was going to shoot you as he thought you had a gun in your hand. You dropped what was in your hand, which turned out to be a screwdriver, and took off running and the officer could see that you was a Juvenile and he was sure glad he had not fired his weapon.

Needless to say the boy's parent almost died when they heard this and the boy finally went on to write out a statement and confess to everything just as his buddy had done, about his involvement in all the burglaries. I told his parents that I was going to take their son to Youth Hall were I had taken his partner in crime and that the Juvenile Judge would probably release him the next day into their custody. At the Juvenile Court hearing they were both adjudicated to be delinquents and they were ordered to spend 30 days in Youth Hall and then be released on probation until they reached their 18th birthday. As Sergeant Preston of the Yukon use to say to his dog King, this case is CLOSED.

Another case involved the speedy and elusive burglar named Andrew James Roseman. This fellow went around committing burglaries all over the place in broad daylight, not caring if anybody saw him or not. He once stopped and talked to a mailman delivering mail to the house he had just burglarized. I was able to identify him by his fingerprints that he left at several burglaries. I had filed several charges against him with the State Attorney's Office and warrants had been issued for his arrest.

One day he was stopped by a motorcycle officer from my department, "Robert E", and when this officer ran a check on him and found out he was wanted on my warrants that had been filed. Having no place to put him being on a motorcycle, he decided to handcuff him and have him sit on the sidewalk until he could have a uniform car come by to transport him to jail. As he approached the subject, the subject took off running from "Robert E". The funny part was that he was running backwards so he could keep his eye on the officer in case he started to shoot or something. Needless to say he out ran "Robert E" and got away, that day. Andrew was later caught, tried and convicted and sent to Raiford prison. A couple of years later "Robert E" made Sergeant and became my partner in Northwest District GIU.

The Northwest District had been plagued with a series of burglaries being committed by an African male and female team hitting houses and stealing TV sets in broad daylight. On e day at roll call, "Robert E" and myself was kidding around with some of the younger detectives (patrolmen) and told them they had one week to catch the two or we would go out and catch them. Well a went by and they were still at large and still breaking into houses. So today we, still kidding around, we told them that we will just have to go out and capture them today as your time is up. As if we wrote a movie scrip, "Robert E" and myself were out on patrol in the area of the burglaries, headed east on Northwest 119th Street approaching Northwest 7th Avenue, when the dispatcher advised of a burglary in progress on Northwest 117th Street between Northwest 7th Avenue and Northwest 10th Avenue. We both thought at the same time that this was too good to be true.

As we approached the house the male was behind the wheel of the vehicle and the female was putting a TV set in the trunk. Their vehicle was facing ours. We got out of our vehicle with guns drawn and told them to put up their hands. The female did but the male, gunned the engine and headed straight for me. I dove out of the way and the vehicle hit a mailbox on top of a concrete post and demolished it.. The vehicle kept on going down the street and I fired two shots trying to disable the vehicle. I hit the vehicle with both shots but the vehicle continued on down the street. I saw things falling off the vehicle from underneath. The car then went around the corner and I lost sight of the car but it was going slow. I gave chase on foot and when I got around the corner there was the car but no subject. A man was standing on his front porch pointing and yelling that he went that way.

   I went to the next corner and another person told me that the subject in in the backyard across the street from his house. As I got around back I saw the subject trying to break in the back door of the house. I took him into custody. "Robert E" could not believe it when I came back to the scene with the subject in custody. He yelled I knew you were fast but how did you run down the car? I let him wonder for awhile and then told him that the car had fallen apart. It was later found out that it was a front wheel drive vehicle, and when it had hit the mailbox and pole it tore the front wheel drive up, hence it stopped when it did. Sure enough it was the two subjects we had been looking for. We rubbed it in on the other detectives for weeks. We told them that when ever they got stumped to call us.

   One of the areas we had Jurisdiction over was called the Strip. It mainly was one road called Collins Avenue, which was also known as A1A and ran north from Bal Harbour at the Haulover Bridge. There was a large County owned and run Park which during WWII was a military beach. It was used by servicemen stationed in the Hotels and Motels on Miami Beach during the war. I had an uncle that had been stationed there before he was shipped over seas. From this Park north there was nothing but Motels,Hotels, shops and restaurants all the way to the City of Surfside. A good friend of mine an former co-worker, Fred Maas, is the present day Chief of Police there.

   One night I was dispatched to a motel on a burglary call where a man had been shot. When I arrived I was met by a man who identified himself as the bodyguard for FATS DOMINO, who was staying and playing a gig in the lounge of this motel. He told me that Fats had forgotten something in his room on the fifth floor and had sent him back to get it. He stated that when he open the door, he was accosted by a white male who after hitting him turned and headed out the sliding glass doors on the balcony. He told me that fearing the burglar was armed, he fired one shot and hit the subject as there was blood on the balcony. He said the subject then climbed up to the next balcony and that was the last he saw of the subject. The subject had climbed up from balcony to balcony and entered Fats room through the sliding glass doors. I started searching the hallways with uniformed officers and in the north stairwell there laid a man with a gunshot wound to his ankle, which also had broken his ankle. Upon searching the subject a pair of Diamond cuff links that spelled out FATS in diamonds were found I his pocket. This made for an easy arrest and conviction in the case. For years I had managed to keep some autograph pictures with Fats holding the diamond cuff links. Some how over the years they have gotten lost.

I will never forget the time when my partner at the time, that my partner at the time, Sergeant J. B. Johnson, said he needed a storage shed for his house and that he had purchased one from a man in Carol City. The only problem was it was used and all assembled. "JB" asked me to help him move this storage shed to his house about 20 blocks from were he bought it. I told him sure I would help him. I didn't know at the time I had said yes, what I was in for. It turned out that :JB" had borrowed a pickup truck and he wanted to put the shed across the back of the pickup truck and move it down the road. He wanted me to follow him in a squad car as an escort would do. I was not too keen on the idea but went along with the idea. We got the shed loaded without any problems, except we had nothing to tie it down with. "JB" said it would be okay if he drove really slow so off we went. You can guess what happened. If you guessed it fell off the truck you win the jackpot. A gust of wind hit the shed and it came flying back at my squad car. I was lucky that it missed the squad car but the shed did not fair as well. We picked up the pieces and took them to his house. We sure got lucky on that one.

Our police Station in Carol City was half Police Station and half Fire Station. One day while I was going over some cases and making some telephone contacts, another Detective, Buck Woolridge was also in the office making telephone calls. He yelled for somebody to go get a fireman as something was on fire as he could smell smoke. Something was burning alright, he was smoking a cigarette and his eyes were watering and he was yelling , "Somethings on fire". I then politely informed him that he was on fire as he had dropped hot ashes on his tie and it had caught fire. It took quite awhile for him to get over that one with all the pranks played on him for a few weeks.

In 1968, a black eye was laid upon the Public Safety Department during an investigation into the illegal Bolita (Lottery) operations in Dade County. The investigation centered around a formed Deputy Sheriff Charles Richard Celona, who had been fired for accepting bribes by some of the known Bolita Operator with in Dade County. The investigation also spread out to include illegal abortions, gambling and prostitution. An investigation by Public Safety Department culminated in the return of numerous indictments as a direct and indirect result of the Celona testimony. It was good that we were cleaning our own house.

They included the indictment of 8 former Deputy Sheriffs or other Law Enforcement personnel. In addition, certain direct informations were file by the assigned State Attorney against other Law Enforcement personnel. These indictments and charges related to the acceptance of bribes and other abuses of the public trust placed in these officers. The Grand Jury returned indictments against 9 alleged Bolita Operators for crimes and conspiracies relating to bribery and corruption of public officials. The Grand Jury also indicted 5 operators of public establishments which allegedly conducted "B" Girl and prostitution operations for crimes involving, bribery and the corruption of public officials. In addition to the indictments returned by the Grand Jury, certain direct indictments were filed by the Assigned State Attorney. One of these involved a burglary of goods valued in excess of $500,000.00 which was thwarted as an indirect result of the Celona Investigation. An indictment is no more and no less than the formal charge by which the people of a community bring the charged party before a duly constituted court and jury for determination of guilt.

The Grand Jury also recommended that those indicted not be prosecuted by the Sate Attorney for the Eleventh Judicial Circuit for several reasons. One being that the public media has often created an air of suspicion about the conduct of certain prosecutions. If, as is possible in any prosecution, some of these cases were to be lost in Court, the State Attorney for the Eleventh Judicial Circuit might again be the subject of innuendos. The Grand Jury recommended that the Celona aspect of this investigation be concluded as quickly as possible.

On October 29, 1964, the New York's American Museum of natural History was broken into by Alan Kuhn, Roger Clark and Jack (Murf The Surf) Murphy. Murphy got the nick name, having recently won a surfing title in Hawaiian Surfing Contest. They committed the largest burglary this country had even seen. They stole the J. P. Morgan Collection of Jewels. This collection included the Star of India Diamond, the Eagle Diamond, the midnight Sapphire and the De Long Ruby. The Star of India Diamond was a 563 carat diamond. Well things might have went extremely well during the burglary but they were arrested within 48 hours in Miami, where they had planned the burglary at the Cambridge Hotel, where a bellhop tipped the police. The Star of India Diamond was recovered in a locked in the downtown Miami Greyhound bus station. Most of the other jewelry they had stolen was recovered except for a few jewels they had already pawned for some ready cash.

It was known to the Miami beach Police that the three of them were pulling off many burglaries all along the beach front at places like The Castaways, The Dunes, The Golden Strand, The Sahara and The Tropicana motels. Jack Murphy and Alan Kuhn were arrested after Ava Gabor saw their pictures on TV and identified them as the ones that had forced their way into her apartment, beat her up pretty badly and stole over $50,000.00 in jewelry. When Ava Gabor did not show up at their trial because she was too busy, the charges were dropped.

Murphy along with two others also broke into the home of Millionaire Olivia Wofford and made her open up a wall safe and in doing so she managed to trip a silent alarm which brought the police down in full force. They made the arrest of the two with Murf but he dove through a plate glass window and escaped. He later was arrested and taken to have his face sewn up from cuts received when the plate glass window broke.

After this Murphy was arrested when he was caught while he and an accomplice conned two women into stealing some securities for them and then the two, Murf and his partner, drowned the two women and weighted their bodies down and dumped them in Whiskey Creek in Fort Lauderdale. When he went to trial he eventually was found to be insane and was committed to the State Mental Hospital. When he was release from the mental hospital all the inmates lined up an sang a Hymn as he had found religion while there.

Being involved with Little League Baseball from the start of my police, sometimes spilled over into mu personal life. One of my 13 year old players, had a brother that had been in some minor trouble as her was running around with the wrong crowd of teenagers. On this day, I had to arrest my player's brother on burglary charges. I attempted to help his brother out as much as I could, but this is the thanks I got.

At this time in my life, I owned a 1964 Nova Station Wagon. It needed a paint job badly. I had found a place, near by my station that did really good paint jobs at reasonable prices. I had my wife drive the car to the paint shop. They really did a nice job painting my car. I looked nice and I was proud of the job they had done. My wife picked up the car and was on her way home and as she was making a proper left turn, a car attempted to pass her and sideswiped the whole side of the car. As fate would have it, the person driving the vehicle that side-swiped my wife happened to be my player's brother. I could not believe it and I did not want to think he had done this on purpose. When this boy and his parents appeared in Juvenile Court on the Burglary Charge, they tried to convince the Juvenile Judge that I had set up the accident. I could hardly believe what I was hearing in Juvenile Court. I was there to ask the Judge on this boy's behalf, that he be placed on probation for his part in the burglary charge. I found out then and there it does pay to try and help some people. The worst part of the deal was that I had to take my car back to the guy who had just put on a beautiful paint job. As I pulled the car into his shop he just stood there shaking his head. He told me kiddingly that if I didn't like the paint job all I would have had to do was tell him. The car was repainted and once again looked beautiful. My player quit my team, even though I was able to convince the Juvenile Judge to place his brother on probation.

I continued coaching Little League until 1970 when I became President of North Miami National Little League. People often asked my how I had the time to do all this and I would say if you want to do something you will find the time. This worked out well while being a plain clothes detective as I could make some contacts while riding around investigating cases. Then I became District Administrator for Little League Baseball District 8. This

District Administrator supervised the operations in all the Little Leagues in Dade, Monroe and South Broward Counties.

When my son became a junior varsity baseball player at Northwest Christian Academy, I was very proud. I tried to attend most all of his games and I noticed that sometimes there would be only one umpire show up to call the game and at other times they would have to ask parent to come out of the stand and umpire the game. When I inquired about this with the High School Athletic Association Officials, they explained that there was a shortage of umpires and that the bigger school varsity games were assigned umpires first and then all the other games had what was left to be used. So being a glutton for more punishment I became a registered High School Umpire and asked to be assigned mostly to the smaller school games in hopes that would help out with the umpires shortage. This helped but I often had to umpire a game by myself. This led me to having to umpire some of my son's games. I umpired high school games for the next four years.

As I stated before being a deputy sheriff came in hardy some times, even while umpiring. Once while umpiring a ball game at Dade Christian High School, I was forced to eject two players from the home team for unsportsmanlike conduct. Needless to say Dade Christian went on to lose the game and made the situation a little more hostile towards myself. As I was leaving the field one of the coaches for Dade Christian came running at me and grabbed my arm and swung me around. He started yelling and cursing and really showing out. I informed him that I was a Deputy Sheriff and that if he put his hands on me again that he would spend the night in the County Jail and be charged with assault. He backed off but continued following me to my vehicle, shouting you will never umpire a game ever again here at his school. I filed a report with the Florida High School Athletic Association and the school was fined $500.00 for the coach and players conduct. If you know me, you would know that I asked for the next game at Dade Christian and was given the game. When I arrived the coaches and the players were surprised to see me. Then I received a surprise when the coaches and all the players came over and shook my hand and apologized to me for their previous conduct.

One thing I could never get resolved was what happen to Detective Neil Lett. Detective Lett was shot one day by a young punk, who was in and out of trouble from the time he was 11 years old. Detective Lett attempted to stop him and question him about some burglaries in and around Westview Junior High School. When Detective Lett stopped the subject in his vehicle,the subject got out of his vehicle and shot Detective Lett several times and got back in his vehicle and fled the scene. Before Detective Lett passed out from his gun shot wounds, he was able to advise the dispatcher who had shot him. The boys name was l\Larry McFarlane. I was in the area and I knew were the subject hung out so I started searching the neighborhood. I was able to locate where the subject was hiding and I entered the house. From the way Detective Lett sounded, I was afraid he was going to died at any moment. I was expecting a possible gun fight from the subject but instead I found him passed out on an overdose of drugs in a bed, in an attempt to take his own life. I took him into custody an sent him via Randall-Eastern Ambulance to the prison ward at Jackson Memorial Hospital. I thought that some day I might at least get a thank you from Detective Lett if he survived. Well he survived his wounds after a long struggle with his wounds and was able to return to duty with the department. But still today I believe that he holds a grudge against me for not killing the subject that shot him. I tried on several occasions to explain that I could not just shoot and kill a passed out unarmed man and live with myself. I would have been a lower scum than McFarlane, but Lett didn't ever want to hear that. He just wanted him dead for having shot him and leaving him for dead.

We did lose a very fine officer Sims Arrington, one day when he responded to a domestic violence call about five blocks from the station. As he pulled up on the scene, without any warning the husband shot him in cold blood. I don't know if the subject ever knew that Sims was an officer as he was in plain clothes in a plain car. I remember the day so well as I was at the Internal Revenue Service Office being audited when Sims was gunned down. When the agent heard the call he told he to go that I kept good records and my taxes were correct, he also wrote that on my file and that must have helped as I have never been audited since.

After a few years at Station 1 G.I.U., station 6 was built at 15665 Biscayne Boulevard. I now understand that they call this station Interama Station. This station sat on County owned property and between our station and Biscayne Bay was a good old smelly, at times, County Dump. They called it a waste facility. Captain Robert Senk was chosen to be the Officer in Charge of the station and Lieutenant Irving Nehr was chosen to be the Office in Charge of G.I.U. At the station. I was approached by them and asked to become the Administrative Sergeant for the new G.I.U., at the station and I accepted the position. I almost thought I had made a mistake when I started ordering and staffing the new offices with furniture and supplies. It was mid summer and the work had to be done before the station could be open and receive the Certificate Of Occupancy. The last thing being installed to the building was the air conditioning system. At least I did not have to wear a cost and tie without cool air. It was shorts and tee shirts. It was always almost 100 degrees in the building that had very few windows and none that opened. This was to make the building very energy efficient. The supplies got ordered and stored, the furniture was in and the telephones, copiers and computers were installed and up and working. A group of detectives were assembled from those officers that had applied for transfer and some that were just transferred to fill the Station's roster.

A couple of years after the station opened, the County decided to build and open a Chlorine Transfer Station right across Biscayne Boulevard from the station. It was put there along the Atlantic Coastline railroad tracks for use by the County Waste Management facility right behind our station. If a leak ever happened it could possible wipe out an entire police station. We were told be happy don't worry that can't happen. As it would turn out this was to be my last duty station until I retired in 1985 after 25 years of service. Station 6 was supposed to be the state of the arts building which included a Heliport, a complete garage and maintenance facility, a mini holding facility, A three shift Uniform Unit and then soon after it was opened a Regional Commander's Office.

As the second in command in G.I.U., I would often work as the night time supervisor when certain operations called for it. One such operation would be a prostitution Sting, which meant the round up of hookers along Collins Avenue. These would come about because of complaints from motel and other business owners. The prostitutes would walk the street picking up prospective Johns (clients). I remember one such time when a Miami Herald reporter wanted to ride along to gather information for the story he was writing about the problem. I took the reported with me so that I could make sure he stayed within the boundaries that I had set for him. Some of the boundaries included that he could not take any facial pictures of prostitutes, their clients or undercover police officers. Also he could not use any information received by an officer in identifying any of the subjects arrested without their permission. Nor could he personally interview any of the subjects arrested with out their permission. He had to put this in writing along with an agreement to hold the Department and any Officer Liable if he was hurt while out with us on this assignment.

It would at times be amusing. We observed a motor home pull up to three or four prostitutes and three or all four managed to get inside the motor home. The motor home went down tooting the air horn as a sign that he had made a score. We followed them back across Sunny Isles Boulevard to a movie theater parking lot. It was a cool night and you could see the windows starting to fog up and the motor home rock from side to side. After about 35 minutes the motor home went back to Collins Avenue were it was stopped and filed interrogation cards and all inside for future reference. As it turned out there were two men and three ladies of the night inside. The two men inside were given citations to appear in court on a charge of procuring for prostitution. The three ladies were arrested for soliciting for prostitution and taken to the County Jail for booking and warnings not to return to the area.

The purpose for doing it this way was to get the hookers off the street for the rest of the night and not to embarrass the males. I always personally believed that both should have gotten the ride to jail to try and stop some of this activity, but was told to handle this type of operation in this manner. I guess it was best as it sure could have caused some real problems, I guess, for a Baptist Minister and a Catholic Priest that night. We arrested a total of 23 Hookers that night and cited 15 Johns. Some of the officers would go inside bars and sit and sip a drink and await to be approached by a Hooker. Since I was not a drinker, I would have been spotted for a cop right away, if I sat there sipping a soda.

Another time that I went along as a supervisor, was with our Vice Squad on a Narcotics buy and bust. This involved a cool $225,000.00, for which I has to check out and sign for it at the Federal Reserve Bank. I made sure, if I could not keep it in my possession, I was going to make sure I could have a good seat, where I could follow where the money car went at all times. This entailed that I be the spy in the sky in our fixed winged Stoll aircraft. This airplane was so neat. It could fly slow or fast and was very quiet. In Miami it is very easy to get around if you know the four points of a compass. Miami is divided into four sections. Northwest, Northeast, Southeast and Southwest with Flagler Street being the north south divider and North Miami Avenue being the east west divider. As the buy car did not know exactly where the buy was to take place until they received the word, we would have to follow it until they received the location of the buy. To disguise any radio transmissions, I informed all on the detail to report locations exactly ten blocks north from where they actually where. And for the final wrinkle, I was referred to as the Houseboat. Well I was relieved when all went well that night, four drug dealers were are arrested, 3 million dollars worth of cocaine was confiscated and nobody was hurt. The money was returned to the bank intact and I was off the hook.

   I believe it was in the early 1970's that I started to become dissatisfied with Miami and South Florida in General. Miami was a great place to live when I arrived as a 14year old teenage. It was a picnic on the beach every Sunday and more swimming at Haulover Beach during the summer. I could ride the Metro Transit over to Haulover Beach from in front of the trailer park where I lived for a dime. I still have a dime token from the Miami Transit Company. As a matter of fact you could ride all over Dade County for a dime each way.

   After graduating from William Jennings Bryan Junior High, I went on to Miami Edison Senior High School and graduated from Miami Edison Senior High School in June 1953. One of the highlights, from my High School years, was the first ever Victory over Miami Senior High School, in forty years in football. The games was always played on Thanksgiving Evening and always drew a crowd of 74,000 or more fans. Can you believe this for a High School Football game.

   The only other major high school at the time was Miami Jackson Senior High School, which Lee Courso made famous and is still with ESPN.. I still have the paper with the headline, "THE JINX IS DEAD". We were favored to win the ball game for the first time in history. We were anticipating the tearing down of the goal posts in the Orange Bowl Stadium for the first time ever. We had all been warned all week at school, that anyone going on the field after the game would be disciplined and Seniors would not be able to graduate.

As the game was ending all the students saw all the teachers gathering along the fence close to one end zone. They sent us the word that if we did not tear the goal post down they would do the job for us. We did the job and we marched from the Orange Bowl through downtown Miami along Flagler Street and threw the goal posts into Biscayne Bay. We went back the next day and retrieved them at took them to our school. After the parade through town we all went back to the school and built a bonfire in the intersection of Northwest 2nd Avenue and Northwest 62nd Street right under the traffic light. When firemen arrived to put out the fire, the keys to the fire truck were thrown down the storm drain. The GOAL POSTS were later planted in the patio of what is now the Old Miami Edison Senior High School. Several players from that team went on to college and some to pro football A few also ended up on, you guessed it, The Public Safety Police Department, now The Miami-Dade Police Department,Jimmy Green and Richard Albright were two of them. Those were the good old days.

Now , back to my losing my love for Miami Dade County. My wife went to the Dentist one day at Northwest 27th Avenue and the Palmetto By-Pass. As she left the dentist office she was mugged in the parking lot by three teenage black males. They knocked her down and drug her a few feet until she let go of her purse. The worst part is that there was an armed black female Security Guard in the parking lot who stood by laughing at the whole thing. There is a doctor's office in one half of the building and the other half was my wife's dentist. My wife was taken into the doctor's office and they refused to give her any time of first aid, they said they didn't want to get involved out of fear of retaliation from the black males. Two detectives that I worked with happened to be in the area and went to her aid. As a result of this attack, my wife never had full use of her left arm again.

Her stolen credit cards were use twice at a Chevron Gas Station at Northwest 27th Avenue and Opa Locka Boulevard. After the second time it was used, I personally responded to that station and made sure they knew that the card was stolen. I told them that if they ever allow it to be use again there I would have them arrested for possession of stolen property based on the use and aiding and abetting a fraud. The card was never used again and I am sorry to say that this was one case that was never solved.

Later on, my home was broken into twice, once while I was on vacation and my next door neighbor was supposed to be looking out after my home and the other while I was in Church one Wednesday evening. On one of the burglaries, I suspected one of the three boys that lived next door and ran around with my son and had even been on vacation with us. The reason I suspected him is because the only things taken was from my son's bedroom. This boy during another time I was on vacation, broke into a house across the street from his and mine, where he raped and murdered the elderly lady that he always mowed the lawn for. He was sent into Juvenile Detention until he was 21 and then released. The second break I feel was committed by a teenage, I had taken into my home as a foster Child, and had left my home. Thats another story in its self about becoming Foster parents. After these two burglaries I made mu home like a fort by putting security screens on the inside of all my jalousie windows to protect what was left that had not been taken as well as for the safety for my family. If the house had ever caught fire and I needed to break a window to get out, I would never have been able to do so. So for these along with higher property taxes and school taxes to pay for the influxation from Cuba, made me to start planning on leaving Miami as soon as I could retire in 1985.

After doing quite a bit of research, I discovered that I could live on about half of what I would need to remain retired and in Miami, so it would be off to North Carolina when I retired. In 1979 I started building my retirement home outside of Murphy, North Carolina. In a little Community called UNAKA which is Cherokee Indian for white man. The first year I had the land cleared and the septic system put in and poured the footers. From then on this became my project every summer vacation time for the next five years. Now back to police work.

Right in the heart of the City of North Miami Beach (which I could never understand why it did not belong to North Miami beach) stood the 163rd Street shopping Center which was unincorporated Dade County, hence Merto-Dade's jurisdiction. The shopping center was a beehive of activity and for a long time my department had two detectives assigned just to the shopping center. One of the biggest problems was shoplifting, followed by purse snatching and strong-armed robberies. With The North Miami Beach Senior High School sitting right across the street from the shopping center fights, along with other crimes and mischief that delighted teenagers, would take place.

One case that came out of the shopping center, came from Mayor's Jewelry Store, renown all over the world for its fine custom jewelry and fine watches. One day a man walked into Mayor's and when he left it was discovered that over $225,000.00 in diamonds and jewelry were missing. After looking at the surveillance tapes over and over it was determined or concluded that a woman clerk, in the store was sen passing something to this man, just before he left the store. Just moments before this she had emerged from the back room where the safe was located and had contained the items now missing. Of course in questioning her she denied knowing the man and stated that she has just been showing him different pieces of jewelry and ended up selling him a watch and she produced a sales slip to prove the watch sale. It took some many days of leg work but since we had his name and address on the sales slip, we started checking for any possible link between the two. We got a break when we obtained three or four months of each of their telephone records. We were then able to prove that at least they knew each other as there were several phone calls between the two of them going back months. After putting a surveillance on both of them, we found out that they and a third party got together very often. Using a court ordered phone tap we monitored the phone calls of all three subjects. During one such monitoring. It was over heard that they were planning a trip to Canada, which we supposed was to dispose of the jewelry. I notified the Royal Canadian Mounted Police of what I suspected and gave a physical description on all three subjects and their vehicle they were traveling in. When they crossed into Canada as part of a routine border check, the entire vehicle and three subjects were searched and no jewelry was found. We gave it our best shot but this tipped our hand that we suspected them and from then on they were very careful not to be seen together nor call each other.

I was ordered by my Station Commander to stop all the overtime it was taking to keep tabs on all three subjects, unless something new in the way of a good lead, was obtained. I sent out fliers on all the jewelry and pictures of some, to all police agencies. I thought that this would be the last I would hear on the case, But low and behold I was sitting in the office one day a few weeks later and it was a Detective from Palm Beach County. He asked if I was still looking for some diamonds and jewelry and I told him I sure was. He told me that if I would come to his station, that he just might have and return some of the stolen diamonds to me.

When I arrived at the Palm Beach County Sheriff's Office, low and behold there laid almost $125,000.00 of the stolen diamonds. The detective told me I would never believe him when he told me how he had come to recover them. It seems that a religious day care center was having the children make Halloween Cards to take home to their parents and they were pasting these pretty bright stones onto the cards. One of the teachers for some reason thought they looked too real to be fake stones so she called the Sheriff's Office to come and look at the stones. They in turn called me. It was discovered that the father of the prime suspect in the case went through his son's closet to get some clothes to give as a donation for a yard sale the day care center was going to have to raise money. If they only knew what they had been given. The suspects father had removed an old pair of tennis shoes from the closet and the diamonds, unknown to him was wrapped in a sock and stuffed in the toe of the tennis shoe and they fell out at the day care center. What a twist of fate in this case. Sometimes pure luck is needed to solve cases.

When I got back to my station, with the diamonds and other jewelry that was recovered from the fathers house, and had been identified by Mayor's Jewelry Store, I went in to see the Captain. I said captain, do you remember the case you told me to quit wasting all the overtime on. He said yes, why? I told him that I had just recovered over $125,000.00 of the diamonds and jewelry and walked out. The Captain could not wait to make a press release and take credit.

From time to time you would catch a sex case to work. All of the cases that G.I.U. Would handle usually involved Juveniles with Juveniles. They usually involved an older juvenile taking Indecent Liberties with a younger Juvenile. The more serious case were most always handled by the Homicide Unit. One of the first cases I investigated resulted from a burglary investigation. Two juveniles boys, one 15 and the other one 16 years old. I had been called to the home of the 15 year old by his mother. She had found out about the burglary and sex offense. The boy told me that the 16year old talked him into doing a burglary at a the 7 – 11 Store. They stole a bunch of cigarettes and cigars. I asked him why in the world he would jeopardize his whole future with a felon conviction on his record for a bunch of cigarettes and cigars. He told me that the 16 year old was blackmailing him in to doing it with him.

He went on to say that there was a place at Thomas Jefferson Junior High School that had a big group of bushes along a section of the building where nobody could see you if you were behind the bushes. Not thinking what he would say next, I asked happen then. He stated that they would give each other blow jobs. I almost fell off my chair when he said that. After the first time they had smoked there with cigarettes they had gotten other places, the 16 year old told the 15 year old that if he didn't help him break into the 7 – 11 Store he would tell everybody that he was gay. The boy said he did not want this to happen but that he didn't mind what they did and even enjoyed it, so he went along with the 16 year old. The older boy was interviewed and when he found out I had talked to the 15 year old he admitted his part. He begged me not to tell his parents and I told him that I would not but he would. Both boys were cited into Juvenile court on the Burglary charge. Case closed. Of course all the other information had to be included in my report for the Juvenile Court.

Another case that I was called upon to investigate, involved a loud party, during school hours at a house on the corner, across the street from Thomas Jefferson Junior Hight School. On the way to the house I stopped by and picked up "Mr. B" at Thomas Jefferson Junior High School. When we arrived at the house, "Mr. B" went to the front door and I went to the back door as usual. When "Mr. B" knocked on the front door, somebody inside yelled its "Mr. B". Well they could not get out the back door and they could not get out the front door so we went in the house as "Mr. B" knew all of them, except for one. All but the one of them went to his school, so they all were busted for being truants.

As it turned out there were five boys and three girls and it had gotten into a real sex orgy. With boys having sex with girls and boys having sex with boys and girls having sex with girls. There all were between the ages of 12 and 16 years old. It just got out of hand and they were making so much noise they got caught. All of them were cited into Juvenile Court. The one 16 year old is the one that actually lived in the house and his parents were both at work.

I don't know if you are old enough to remember those wonderful S & H Green Stamps that you would lick and stick and put them in the savings books for redemption at a Redemption Center near you for all sort of things. The books also were worth a cash value of $3.00. I forget how many stamps it took to fill a book, but it sure seemed like it would take forever to fill a book. That was a lot of money when they first started out.

Even the thieves knew the value of these stamps. One of the major places you would receive these green stamps from was at your local Margaret Ann/ Kwik-Chek/Winn-Dixie store. A gang had developed that went around all over South Florida, breaking into these stores taking mostly cigarettes and these S & H Green stamps. These burglaries went on for over a year until we got lucky and arrested one of the gang for an armed robbery. He began to talk and was looking for help with his armed robbery case. We asked him what he was willing to do to help us and help himself at the same time and he agreed to let us know the next location and the date and time it was to happen. We agreed to help him out for this information, but reminded him that if he did not come through with the information, that all bets would be off.

It was not too long after we cut him loose, without putting him in jail that he gave us the location of a Kwik-Chek store on Bird Road that they were going to hit. We thought we had it made with this information and set up a stake out and had the store surrounded. We needed however to catch them in the act of trying to break in before we could make a great case against them. They arrived at the appointed date and time and had even gotten out of their van with their tools, when all of a sudden they jumped back into their van and took off leaving all their tools behind. We guess that they didn't want to take a chance of being stopped and being charged with possession of burglary tools or become known to police.

When we caught up with our informant, he told us that a man had turned on his back door light and him and his dog had come out into the back yard. This was the reason they spooked. He then told us they were going to hit a different place. It was to be a plumber's contractor on a Thursday night when the contractor had Friday's cash payroll in his safe in his office. The informant assured us that this was good information, so another stake out was set up. This building sat on a street corner and had an alley running behind the building from this building all the way to the next street. Another alley took off from this alley like a T. Right across the street from the Plumbing Contractors Building on the opposite corner was an Old Age Nursing Home. From the second floor of the Nursing Home you could see the back door of the target building and all the way down the alley as well. Three officers were placed in the Nursing Home, myself and another detective were place where the alley had the T intersection. Two officer were at the other end of the alley. Two other sets of detectives were a couple of blocks away in hidden squad cars along with a uniform police vehicle and two uniformed officers. The detectives in the Nursing Home were getting spooked with all the moaning and groaning that was going on in there.

The subjects arrived at 11:00 pm and broke into the contractors building through the overhead door in the alley. They had their van parked up against the building and it had the plumbing contractor's name painted on it. Everyone was well armed on the stake out team as we were told that the subject were always armed. It was decided to throw some rock at the overhead door to flush out the subjects and ask them to surrender. The rock were thrown and they hit the door and a few seconds later the door went up and out came the subject firing their weapons.

   Two subject came running down the alley towards me and the other detective with me. I was lying prone of the ground for least exposure. I yelled and told they to halt, but one was running straight at me so, I fired one shot of OO buckshot which missed followed by a second round, and I saw this subject fly backwards towards the building. I saw another subject running across the back of the building with buckshots hitting in front and back of him so I assumed he had been shot but he kept on running down the alley being chased by the other detective with me. I told the subject that I had evidently shot to put up his hands over his head. He yelled that he could not that as his arm was broken. About that time another subject jumped over me dropping a bunch of tools and he went flying down the T part of the alley. I yelled that I had somebody on the ground down my way and for somebody to shine some lights down the alley so I could see. Sure enough I had wounded one of them that had shot at me. The one that went down the T alley was caught by some City of Miami Police that had been notified. The other detective that had been with me came walking back with the man he had been chasing in handcuffs. Three other subjects had been arrested at the back door and the three others had that been arrested but wait 7 had gone into the building, so one got away to inform another day. I was glad that I didn't have to fire any more rounds as a casing had gotten stuck in the ejection slot and had made my weapon really useless had I really needed it. I never took an automatic shotgun with me again, only a pump shotgun. That really didn't end the case.

   We served search warrants on all the homes of the subjects looking for the good old S & H green stamps and stolen cigarettes. All the S & H green stamps had serial numbers on them. We had listed the serial numbers from the last three burglaries in the search warrants. We entered the first house and I could not believe what was in the house. Things that were being used and/or just being stored there ,obviously came from a Green Stamp Redemption Store. One closet was filled with womens shoes still in boxes. It was easy to tell they had be obtained with green stamps, but if we could not find evidence in the house to connect the persons in the house to the burglaries there would be nothing we could do about it, nor impound any of the property. We were about to give up hope and hope they, were having better luck at one of the other houses when I opened a dresser drawer, which I assumed also had been obtains with stamps and in the bottom of the second drawer under all the womens underwear was one full page, of those wonderful S & H Green stamps. I yelled out EUREAKA. The stamps matched the serial numbers of the stamps named in the search warrants. We cleaned out the whole house including 125 pairs of womens shoes and everything else except the stove and refrigerator. Thus brought to a close a bunch of Burglaries and the recovery of thousands of dollars worth of property bought with stolen green stamps. The cigarettes taken in the burglaries were later found out to have been sold to an exporter who shipped them overseas to be sold on the Black Market. The subjects all received various prison terms except for the informant, who didn't learn his lesson, and was arrested by the City of Miami on a Burglary charge a short time later.

Since the pay with the County at this time was not that great, I would from time to time work off duty jobs in uniform even though I was a detective. One of the jobs. I really loved, involved working was at Northwest 7th Avenue and Northwest 141st Street and was called THE PLACE. This was great as it was only 3 blocks from my home and made for a short commute time. THE PLACE was a converted old FOOD FAIR grocery store into a teenage dance hall and would feature some of the top bands of the 70's. Every Friday and Saturday they would pack out the place with 300 people, which was all the fire code would allow. I would usually work the front door to keep count and to keep out those that had been drinking or those that were high on drugs. Three officers would be inside walking around the crowd keeping order. I always worried that one of my officers would get assaulted for some reason with it so crowded and we would not be able to get to his aide. Thank goodness this never happened. I did however close the place down one night. A crazy band from the United kingdom set off some railroad fusees on the stage and caught the stage curtains on fire. This resulted in only minor damage and the fire was quickly put out, but I shut the place down and advised the audience that the pace was closed. The owner of the place went wild and came to me and told me I could not do this as they would loose lots of revenue. I called for a Fire Marshall and he not only agreed with me but also fined them $5000.00 as they did not have the proper permits to have any kind of pyrotechnics in the building or show. Needless to say I was not their favorite person to work as security, but they had no say as to which police officers would work this job. Also as a result of this they were also required to hire one additional off duty officer.

One night, one of the workers at THE PLACE, came up to me and stated that the buckets seats had been stolen out of his personal vehicle in the parking lot. I was glad that they supplied the security for the parking lots. This way my Department nor any of the off duty officers could be held liable in any way for thefts out of vehicles which I am sure happened all the time. I requested that an on duty uniform car come by and take the theft report. Several days later I receive a call from the man who had lost the bucket seats. He said I would not believe it but in the process of replacing his stolen bucket seats, he ended up getting his own seat that were stolen back. He stated that his Insurance Company would not pay for new buckets seats so he would have to settle on used seats. He had his Volkswagen at a dealership in West Hollywood and they had somehow obtained his original seats as replacement for the ones that had been stolen. They had obtained these seat over a radio network that buys and sells used auto parts all over Florida.

The seat were shipped from a junkyard in Tampa Florida that swore that they had the vehicle that the seats came out of and sent. Since I could not prove differently nothing could be done unless I got further or other proof. When the man went to inspect the replacements seats he was amazed to find the stains from a strawberry milk shake that his son had spilled in the vehicle before the seats were stolen. Here were the same stains on these seats, how odd. I tried to make a case against the junk yard but was unable to do so just on the stain evidence and the worn statement from the junk yard in Tampa. The thieves were never caught to my knowledge but had his original seats back.

I use to run into cases from time to time that really makes it hard for some honest people to collect on their homeowner insurance policies. I know most insurance companies want their premium payments for the insurance they sell you with all the little loop holes, on their behalf, to hold down what they have to pay out in claims. They sure hate to pay off claims. I arrested a juvenile one time for breaking into several houses between Northwest 149th Street and Northwest 163rd street. He told me each house that he had broken into and everything he took out of each house. What he said about one house did not matched the report. The boy told me he took some fishing tackle and a fishing pole, along with a bicycle used to ride home on. He firmly stated that he never entered the main part of the house. I found that everything he told me match report for report what had been taken in each burglary. The homeowner of this house over and over if everything on his list of stolen property was really taken. He always said yes. I asked about the fishing tackle and fishing rod along with the bicycle that the bot said he stole. I told him the boy never went into the main part of his house and only tool the fishing gear and bicycle to ride home. I told the homeowner that I would write up my report as to the facts as I knew them and he would have to take the rest up with his insurance company. I returned the fishing gear and bicycle to the man. I obtained his homeowners Insurance Company's name and sent them a copy of the report and arrest. I later found out his claim was denied and his homeowners insurance canceled and he would not be able to obtain any further insurance once a report was file with the Insurance Commissioner's Office in Tallahassee.

This was to me like some police officers that would write people tickets for not having a valid inspection sticker on their vehicle and yet have an expired inspection sticker on their own vehicle. I heard a motorcycle officer bragging as to how many inspection sticker tickets he wrote one day. Out in the station parking lot sat his personal vehicle with an expire inspection sticker on it. I put a ticket on it and told the officer, I would do so everyday until it had a valid inspection sticker on it.

Having to arrest people, living in the same community, sometimes would put you in a bind. As a result of this we were allowed to carry firearms while off duty. I carried one at all times as one never knows what might come up. I only got involved a couple of times while I was off duty. Once as I mentioned before was while I was umpiring a high school baseball game. The other time, I was driving along the Palmetto Express Way and came upon a Florida Highway Patrol officer having trouble trying to take two subject into custody and they did not appear that they wished to be taken into custody. I quietly stopped my vehicle on the shoulder of the road and got out and yelled to the officer that I was a Deputy Sheriff and that I had his back. I also told him I was armed and had the subjects covered. At this time the subjects surrendered without further problems.

I guess that I could ramble on and on as things come back to my mind, but maybe I will save them for another time or book.

I feel very proud to have served my Country by serving in the United State Navy, but also my local Community by proudly serving and protecting the Citizens of Dade County Florida. I feel that many, many more young Americans should be come more active in the Federal, State or County governments in some manner as their contribution for living in a FREE society.

One thing that I found out as being a Christian and a police officer at the same time, was that some of your social groups would shun you because you were a police officer and the others would shun you because you were a Christian.

I have nothing but fond memories of my 25 years and two days on the force. We had some great Christmas parties and became a large family that you could count on if you were in trouble. My last day of work was Friday, April 12th , 1985. I was taken to lunch by my co-workers, given a pin and a ball point pen by the County and was presented with a 410 over/under shotgun as a retirement gift from the co-workers. I also had my personal chauffeur all day long to make sure I didn't get involved in anything I might have to go to court later on about and just to keep me out of trouble in general. I played "Lets Go Out In A Blaze Of Glory" all day long on a cassette player. I left work at 4:00 pm and by 6:00 pm I was on my way to my retirement home that I had almost finished outside of Murphy, North Carolina, in a little Co,,unity known as UNAKA. I thank GOD for keeping me safe all these years.

May God continue to Bless Our Nation, and the rights we have obtained and have defended for so many years. The year 2009 showed that anything can happen in a FREE COUNTRY.

YOU ALL TAKE CARE, "YOU HEAR", ITS A JUNGLE OUT THERE!!

Robert J Palmer

25 YEARS WITH Miami-Dade POLICE

Robert J Palmer

Made in the USA
Columbia, SC
16 February 2025